I0819469

INTRODUCTION

Hello, lovely crafter! I'm Rachele and I am so proud to offer you this crochet blanket pattern book. In it you'll find 18 full blanket designs filled with fun, interesting techniques and traditional stitches. I have been crocheting since 2005, and have not skipped a day since I picked up my hook. Over the years my crafty business has evolved and transformed. Most recently, my favorite thing is to look at art, architecture, nature, street murals – anything visually engaging – and imagine a new blanket design. I have published over 120 crochet blanket patterns independently, in bookazines, magazines, and in my first pattern book, *The Art of Crochet Blankets*.

Finding new ways to create modular designs and playing with shape and color have come to define my work, and I decided to create a new volume of blanket patterns to celebrate my signature approach. You will notice that I tend to lend my own "cozy maximalist" twist to the typical motif blanket! If you have followed my work, you will know that I love pushing the limits of crochet design by combining different motifs and stitch patterns in the same blanket, experimenting with scale and structure.

My original inspiration for these geometric extravaganza came from studying fabric quilts. When working with fabric one can simply cut the shapes, but translating that to a crochet pattern comes with its challenges, and I love to be challenged! A blanket's shape is like my canvas, and I use geometry, color theory, knowledge of stitch construction, and other techniques to fill that canvas creatively and create repeatable blanket patterns.

That is the crux of my work: creating art that you, the crafter, can replicate and make your own. This is the goal that I have been working towards as I have developed my skills as a designer. I hope that you find these 18 projects engaging and fun. My goal was to include a mix of quick-and-easy and challenging makes, to offer you new stitches and delight you with familiar ones, all while bringing you bright, bold and opulent designs.

Enjoy and happy crafting!

Rachele

CROCHET MODULAR BLANKETS

18 mixed motif
designs that play
with shape and scale

RACHELE CARMONA

DAVID & CHARLES
— PUBLISHING —

www.davidandcharles.com

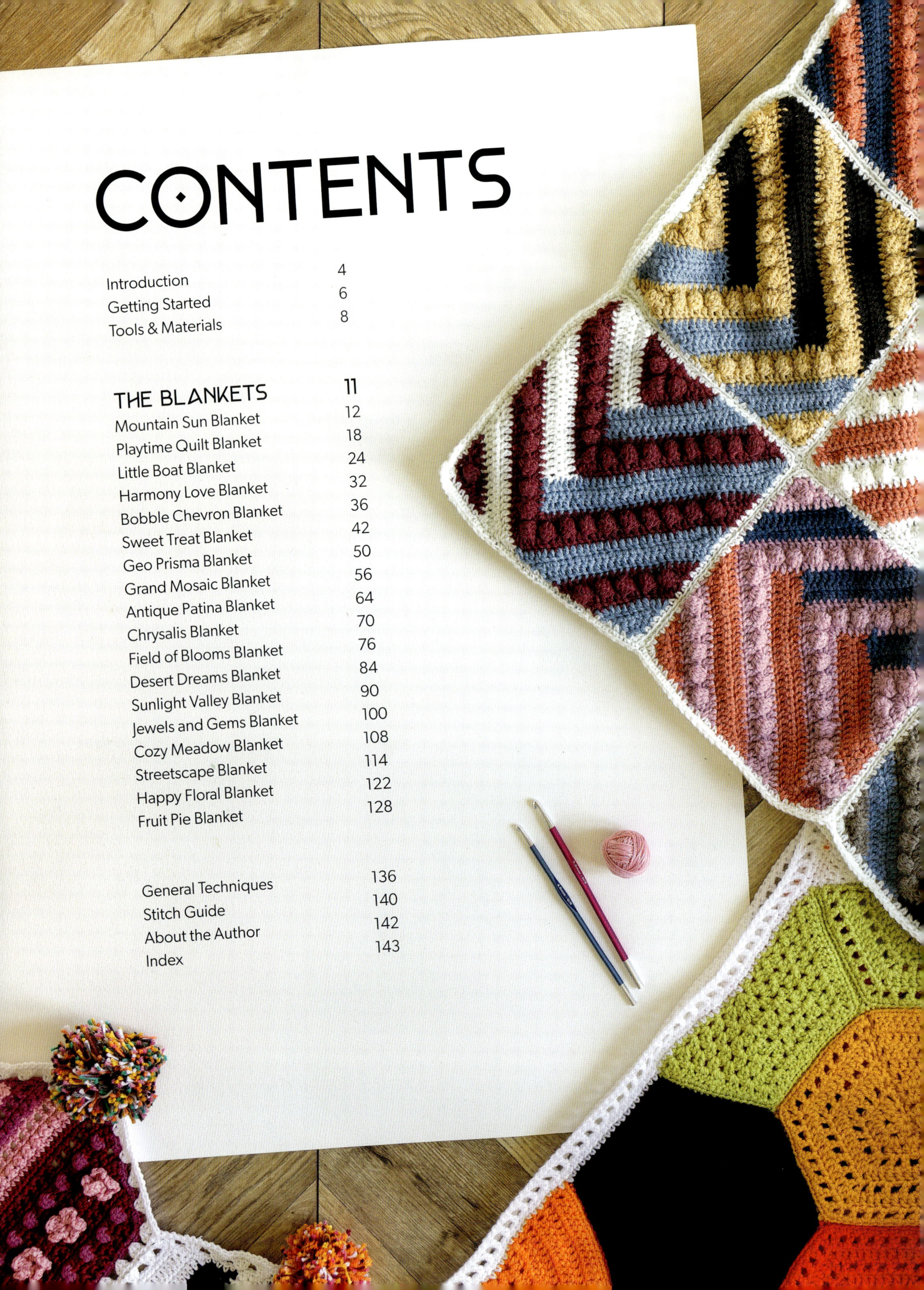

CONTENTS

GETTING STARTED

Gauge (Tension)

Gauge is especially important in modular blankets because you are working motifs, sometimes of different shapes and sizes, that will need to fit together to make the blanket body. The thing that will affect your gauge most of all is how tall your double crochet stitches are.

Ideally, a double crochet stitch should be twice the height of a single crochet stitch. If it is much taller, I suggest practicing to shorten the first loop that you pull up – focus on pulling up just enough yarn to draw the yarn through. Make sure not to loosen up your gauge as you become familiar with the pattern.

If necessary, change your hook size to match the gauge given in the pattern. If your motif is too big, go down a hook size. If it is too small, go up a hook size.

Crochet Terms

This book uses US crochet terms throughout. For a list of abbreviations and techniques, see the Stitch Guide, where you will also find conversions to UK terminology for the stitches used.

Starting a Row Without Chaining

In general, when crocheting you must raise the yarn to the height of the stitch at the beginning of a round. This is often done by "chaining up": ch1 for a single crochet, ch2 for a half double crochet, and so on. You can also use standing stitches.

I use "beginning stitches" when the first stitch of the round is the height of a US double crochet or taller, including any clusters, bobbles, or popcorns. Because the single crochet is a short stitch, I go right into it without chaining up. See the Stitch Guide for instructions and abbreviations for beginning stitches.

The beginning double crochet is my favorite substitute for the first double crochet of the round, as the stitches are very similar. In A, the beginning dc is shown on the left, and a full regular dc is on the right.

Repeats

Square brackets are used for small repeats or consecutively worked stitches, such as "4dc, [2dc, 3tr, 2dc] twice". Asterisks are used for repeats that include small repeats, such as "*5dc, [1ch, 1dc] 3 times in next ch; rep from * 3 times more".

Round brackets are used for multiple stitches worked in the same stitch or space, such as "(3tr, 3ch, 3tr) in next st".

Stitch Counts

Stitch counts are given when the stitch count has changed, in the following format: [12 dc, 3 ch1-sp].

How to Use the Placement Guides, Tables, and Charts in this Book

There are three types of diagrams or charts in the patterns, which tell you different things.

All patterns have a Placement Guide, which shows how to lay out the motifs to make up the body of the blanket. Most Placement Guides are in color to match the yarn color used for each motif. Many also show other information, such as indicating how to orientate different motifs, or the order in which to join the motifs if they are joined with the PLT join (see General Techniques: Joining Methods) as you work.

Some motifs also have a Motif Chart, which is a visual representation of the stitches in the motif pattern that you can use in conjunction with the written instructions. See the Chart Key for details of how each stitch is represented.

A few patterns use many different colors for each motif, or have a few motifs worked in many different colorways. In this case the yarn colors are shown in a Color Table, or sometimes as a Color Guide diagram.

Chart Key

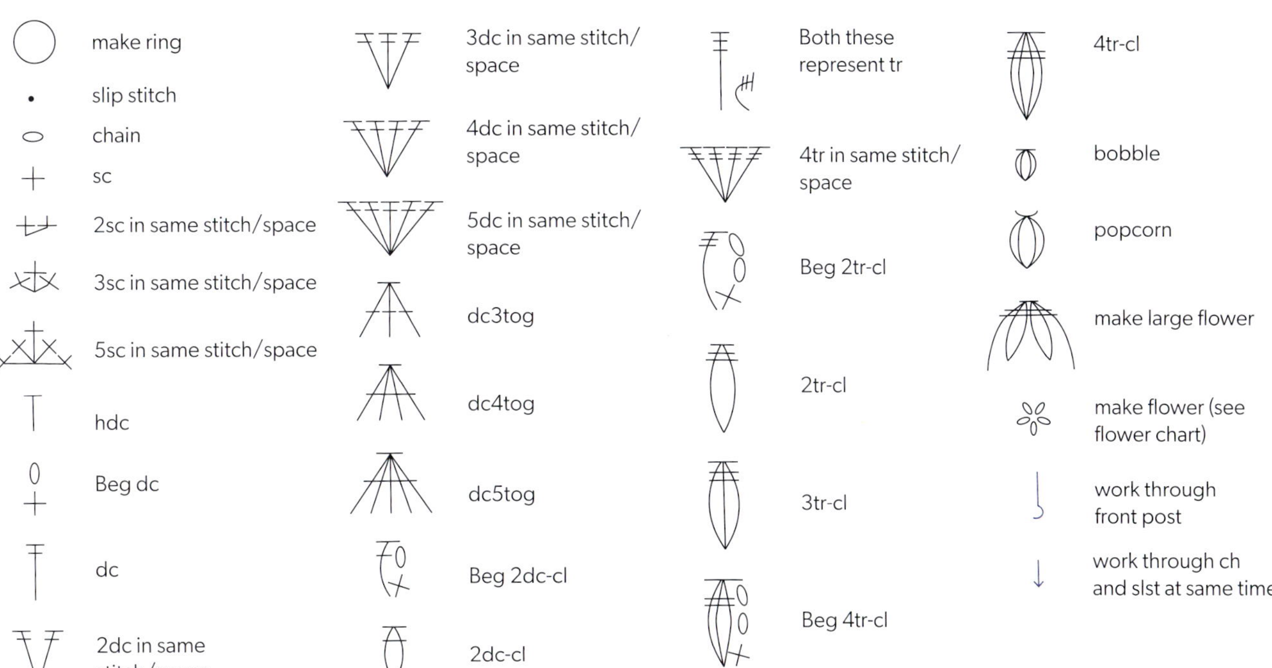

TOOLS & MATERIALS

Yarn

I enjoy working with a variety of yarns of different composition and weight. I design my blankets so that they can be worked up in any yarn or any weight, but you should consider that the yarn weight will affect the final blanket size and weight. For example, thicker yarns will make a blanket heavier and larger, which is sometimes desired, but good to note. In this book I have used a wide assortment of yarns with different aesthetics, makeup, and weight to encourage makers to reach out of their comfort zone and experiment with using different yarns. However, any yarns can be used with my patterns.

Hooks

My favorite crochet hooks are the KnitPro Zing single-end crochet hooks, because I prefer a tapered, lightweight aluminum hook. Any crochet hook can be used, including in-line hooks, or hooks with a cushion grip such as Tulip or Addi brands.

Notions

Scissors

Any crafting scissors can be used, as long as they are sharp and pointed. Dull scissors can fray the yarn, and rounded tip scissors can make it difficult to make a precise cut.

Stitch Markers

For our purposes, I would recommend using locking stitch markers because they will be the easiest to place and remove during the crochet project. Other stitch marker types could snag your work or may be difficult to remove.

Tapestry Needle

Various tapestry needles are available, but for a crochet project I recommend looking for a blunt needle with a large eye and a straight tip. Sharp needles can split the yarn and a small eye is difficult to thread. The straight tip is just my preference, as the bent tip needles will work fine.

Project Bags

When selecting a project bag, it is good to look for features that are geared toward makers. I love it when little things like yarn feeders and notion-holding magnets are included. Divided spaces are also handy for organization, and a convenient shoulder strap is a must for taking your project on the go.

3.0mm
E/4
4.0mm - G/6
4.5mm - 7
5.0mm - H/8

THE
BLANKETS

MOUNTAIN SUN BLANKET

In this piece, I have used some traditional stitch combinations in a fresh, modern way. You will find familiar sunburst motifs worked from corner to corner, and comforting granny stitch worked in a new direction. With a mix of motifs representing the shining sun and bold mountains, this blanket is simple enough that you can work on it while relaxing, but engaging enough that you won't want to put it down.

Finished Size

42 x 42in (107 x 107cm)

Yarn

Worsted (aran) weight (#4 Medium)

Shown here: Berroco Merino 401 (100% extra fine Merino wool), 50g (109yd/100m), 2 balls each in following colors, unless otherwise specified:

- Yarn A: Pearl (11201); 6 balls
- Yarn B: Merlot (11260)
- Yarn C: Gold (11213)
- Yarn D: Strawberry (11239)
- Yarn E: Crepe (11204)
- Yarn F: Teal (11274)
- Yarn G: Denim (11210)
- Yarn H: Graphite (11208)

Hook

- US H/8 (5mm) hook
- US G/6 (4mm) hook for border

Gauge (Tension)

18 dc x 8 rows = 4 x 4in (10 x 10cm) using a US H/8 (5mm) hook.

Pattern Notes

Motifs are completed then joined with Slip-stitch Join (see General Techniques: Joining Methods).

To join new yarns, slst in specified stitch.

Make Blanket Body

Motif 1 (make 8)

Row 1 (RS): With Yarn E, MR, beg dc, 5dc, fasten off, do not turn. [6 dc]

Join Yarn B to first st, ready to work another RS row.

Row 2: Beg tr in first st, ch1, [2tr-cl, ch2] 3 times, 2trcl, ch1, 1tr in final st, fasten off, do not turn. [4 2tr-cl, 2 tr, 3 ch2-sp, 2 ch1-sp]

Join Yarn H to first ch-sp, ready to work another RS row.

Row 3: 2sc in first ch-sp, 3sc in each of next 3 ch-sp, 2sc in final ch-sp, turn. [13 sc]

Row 4 (WS): Beg dc in first st, [2dc in same st, sk2, 3dc in next st] 4 times, turn. [21 dc]

Row 5 (RS): Beg dc3tog, [ch4, dc5tog] 3 times, ch4, dc3tog, fasten off, do not turn. [3 dc5tog, 2 dc3tog, 4 ch4-sp]

Join Yarn G to first st, ready to work another RS row.

Row 6: Beg dc in first st, [3dc, ch1] twice in each of next 3 ch-sp, [3dc, ch1, 3dc] in final ch-sp, 1dc in final st, fasten off, do not turn. [26 dc, 7 ch1-sp]

Join Yarn F to first st, ready to work another RS row.

Row 7: 1sc in first st, [ch3, 1sc in next ch-sp] 7 times, ch3, 1sc in final st, turn. [9 sc, 8 ch3-sp]

Row 8 (WS): 1sc in first st, ch1, [1sc in next ch-sp, ch3] 7 times, 1sc in next ch-sp, ch1, 1sc in final st, turn. [10 sc, 7 ch3-sp, 2 ch1-sp]

Row 9 (RS): 1sc in first st, 1sc in first ch-sp, 3sc in next ch-sp, 3hdc in next ch-sp, 3dc in next ch-sp, (3tr, ch3, 3tr) in next ch-sp, 3dc in next ch-sp, 3hdc in next ch-sp, 3sc in next ch-sp, 1sc in last ch-sp, 1sc in final st, fasten off, do not turn. [6 tr, 6 dc, 6 hdc, 10 sc, 1 ch3-sp]

Join Yarn D to first st, ready to work another RS row.

Row 10 (RS): 1sc in first st, 13sc, 5sc in ch-sp, 14sc, fasten off, turn. [33 sc]

With WS facing, join Yarn C to first st.

Row 11 (WS): Beg dc in first st, 2dc in next st, [sk2, 3dc in next st] 4 times, sk2, 9dc in next st, [sk2, 3dc in next st] 4 times, sk2, 2dc in next st, 1dc in final st, turn. [39 dc]

Row 12: Beg dc3tog, [ch3, dc3tog] 12 times, fasten off, do not turn. [13 dc3tog, 12 ch3-sp]

Join Yarn A to first st, ready to work a RS round.

Border Rnd (RS): 5sc in first st, [3sc in each of next 6 ch-sp, 5sc in next st] twice, 18sc evenly across side to center ring, 5sc in ring, 18sc evenly across side, fasten off and weave in ends. [92 sc]

Motif 2 (make 8)

Work as for Motif 1, using Yarns: C, D, F, G, H, B, E, A.

Motif 1

Motif 3 (make 4)

BASE TRIANGLE

Make 4 in colors shown in Placement Guide.

Row 1 (RS): With Color 1, MR, beg dc, [ch1, 3dc] twice, ch1, 1dc, turn. [8 dc, 3 ch1-sp]

Row 2: 1dc in first ch-sp, [ch1, 3dc in same sp, 3dc in next ch-sp] twice, ch1, 1dc in same sp, turn. [14 dc, 3 ch1-sp]

Row 3: 1dc in first ch-sp, [ch1, 3dc in same sp, 3dc between next 2 groups of 3 dc, 3dc in next ch-sp] twice, ch1, 1dc in same sp, fasten off, turn. [20 dc, 3 ch1-sp]

Row 4: Join Color 2 in first ch-sp, 1dc in same sp, *ch1, 3dc in same sp, [3dc between next 2 groups of 3 dc] to next ch-sp, 3dc in next ch-sp; rep from * once more, ch1, 1dc in same sp, fasten off, turn. [6 dc inc]

Row 5: Rep Row 4. [32 dc, 3 ch1-sp]

Rows 6 and 7: With Color 3, rep Rows 4 and 5. [44 dc, 3 ch1-sp]

WORK ACROSS BASE TRIANGLES

Line up base triangles with RS facing in order shown in Placement Guide. Row 1 is worked across base triangles in order, from right to left.

Join Yarn A in first ch-sp of first triangle.

Row 1 (RS): Beg dc in first ch-sp, ch1, *[3dc between next 2 groups of 3 dc] 6 times, (3dc, ch1, 3dc) in next ch-sp, [3dc between next 2 groups of 3 dc] 6 times, sk last ch-sp; rep from * twice more, once in each base triangle, until final ch-sp of third triangle is reached, ch1, 1dc in final ch-sp of third triangle, turn. [128 dc, 5 ch1-sp]

Row 2: Beg dc in first ch-sp, ch1, *[3dc between next 2 groups of 3 dc] 6 times, (3dc, ch1, 3dc) in next ch-sp, [3dc between next 2 groups of 3 dc] 6 times, sk 6 dc; rep from * twice more ignoring final sk 6 dc, ch1, 1dc in final ch-sp, turn.

Row 3: Rep Row 2, but do not turn.

Join color shown in Placement Guide to first ch-sp, ready to work another RS row.

Row 4 (RS): Rep Row 2.

Rows 5–7: Rep Row 2, turn, do not fasten off. Cont to Square Off Edges.

Motif 3

Square Off Edges

FILL TRIANGLE 1

Cont using same color.

Row 1 (RS): Beg dc in first ch-sp, ch1, [3dc between next 2 groups of 3 dc] until next ch-sp, ch1, 1dc in ch-sp, turn. [20 dc, 2 ch1-sp]

Rows 2–6: Rep Row 1 another 5 times. [5 dc, 2 ch1-sp]

Row 7: Beg dc in first st, 1dc in final st, fasten off and weave in ends.

FILL TRIANGLE 2

Cont using same color, slst in center ch-sp at tip of center base triangle.

Row 1 (RS): Beg dc in first ch-sp, ch1, [3dc between next 2 groups of 3dc] until center 6 dc, sk 6 dc, [3dc between next 2 groups of 3 dc] until final ch-sp, ch1, 1dc in final ch-sp, turn. [38 dc, 2 ch1-sp]

Rows 2–6: Rep Row 1 another 5 times. [8 dc, 2 ch1-sp]

Row 7: 1dc in final ch-sp, fasten off and weave in ends.

FILL TRIANGLE 3

Cont using same color, slst in center ch-sp above rightmost base triangle and work as for Fill Triangle 2.

FILL TRIANGLE 4

Cont using same color, slst in first ch-sp of Row 7 of Fill Triangle 3 and work as for Fill Triangle 1.

With RS facing, join Yarn A to top right cnr sp. On this round, work into side of dc sts as if they were ch-sps.

Motif Border Rnd: 5sc in cnr sp, [2sc in each of next 2 sp, 3sc in next sp] 10 times, 2sc in next sp, 3sc in each of next 7 sp, 5sc in cnr sp, [2sc in next sp, 3sc in next sp] 6 times, 2sc in next sp, 5sc in cnr sp, [31sc across base triangle edge] 3 times, 5sc in cnr sp, [2sc in next sp, 3sc in next sp] 6 times, 2sc in next sp, slst in first sc, fasten off and weave in ends. [270 sc]

Motif 4 (make 2)

Rnd 1 (RS): With Yarn E, MR, beg dc, 15dc, slst in beg dc, fasten off. [16 dc]

Rnd 2: Join Yarn B to any st, beg 2tr-cl in same st, [ch2, 2tr-cl] 15 times, ch2, slst in beg 2tr-cl, fasten off. [16 2tr-cl, 16 ch2-sp]

Rnd 3: Join Yarn D to any ch-sp, 3sc in each of 16 ch-sp, slst in first sc. [48 sc]

Rnd 4: Beg dc in next st, [4dc in same st, sk2, 1dc in next st] 16 times, omitting final dc on last rep, slst in beg dc. [80 dc]

Rnd 5: Beg dc5tog, [ch4, dc5tog] 15 times, ch4, slst in beg dc5tog, fasten off. [16 dc5tog, 16 ch4-sp]

Rnd 6: Join Yarn A to any ch-sp, [5sc, ch1] in each of 16 ch-sp, slst in first sc. [80 sc, 16 ch-sp]

Rnd 7: Slst in next 2 sts, 1sc in same st, [ch3, 1sc in next ch-sp, ch3, sk2, 1sc] 16 times, omitting final sc on last rep, slst in first sc. [32 sc, 32 ch3-sp]

Rnd 8: Slst in first ch-sp, 1sc in same ch-sp, [ch3, 1sc in next ch-sp] 31 times, ch3, slst in first sc. [32 sc, 32 ch3-sp]

Rnd 9: [3sc in each of next 3 ch-sp, 3hdc in next ch-sp, ch1, 3dc in next ch-sp, ch1, (3tr, ch3, 3tr) in next ch-sp, ch1, 3dc in next ch-sp, ch1, 3hdc in next ch-sp] 4 times, slst in first sc, fasten off. [24 tr, 24 dc, 24 hdc, 36 sc, 16 ch1-sp, 4 ch3-sp]

Rnd 10: Join Yarn A to any cnr ch-sp, [5sc in cnr sp, 31sc] 4 times, slst in first sc, fasten off and weave in ends. [144 sc]

Motif 4

Motif 5 (make 2)

Work as for Motif 4, using Yarns: D, B, E, B, A.

Join Motifs

Arrange Motifs 1 and 2 as shown in Placement Guide, and join using Slip-stitch Join (see General Techniques: Joining Methods) through BLO, holding motifs with WS together and working across horizontal seams. Rotate work and join across vertical seams until all motifs are joined.

Border Rnd: Join Yarn A to any cnr st, [3sc in same st, 23sc across 1 motif, 24sc across next 2 motifs, 23sc across 1 motif] 4 times, slst in first sc. [388 sc]

With Yarn A, join Motifs 3, 4, and 5 to blanket body, joining across 2 horizontal seams and 2 vertical seams, working from one edge of blanket to other. Weave in all ends and work blanket border.

Make Blanket Border

With RS facing and larger hook, join Yarn A to any cnr st.

Rnd 1: [3sc in cnr st, 1sc in each st to next cnr] 4 times, slst in first sc, fasten off and weave in ends.

Change to smaller hook.

Rnd 2: [3sc in cnr st, 1sc in each st across to next cnr st] 4 times, slst in first sc, fasten off and weave in ends.

Finishing

Weave in any rem ends and block blanket to given measurements and to flatten seams.

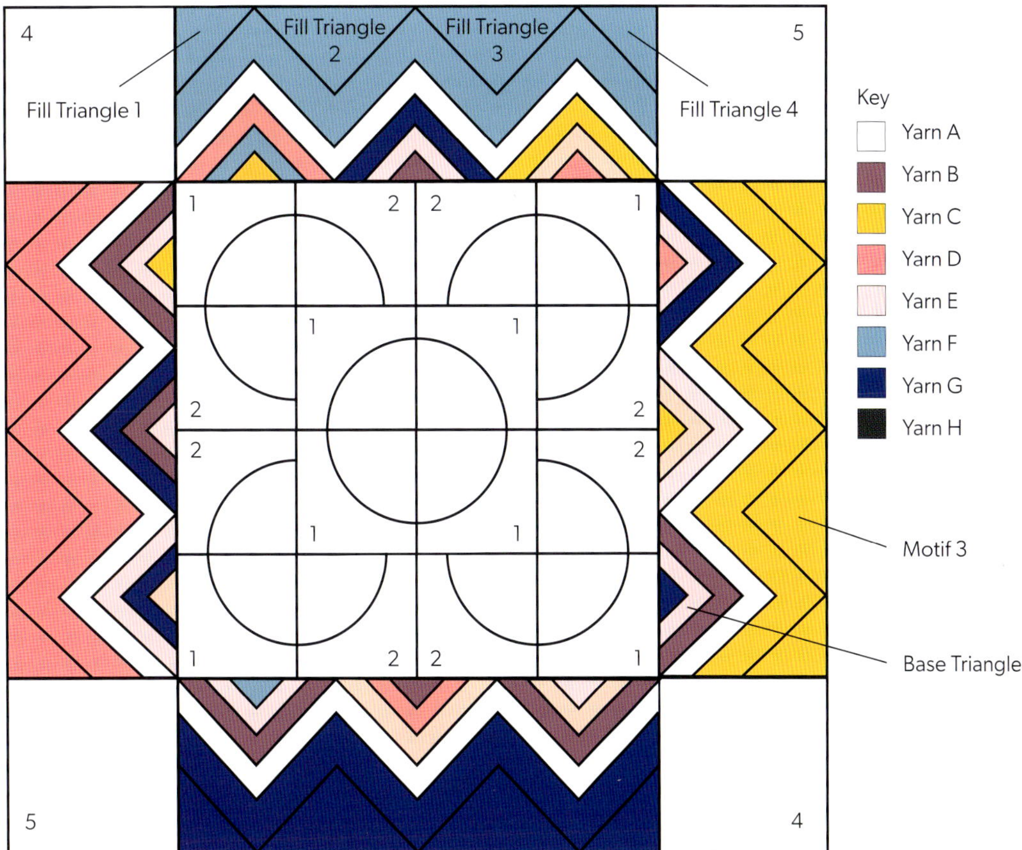

PLAYTIME QUILT BLANKET

This blanket is a play on fabric quilting. The main motifs emulate cutting half-square triangles from different fabrics to make a block, and the chevron motifs are a riff on using sashing to border the squares on a quilt. Whether you use the colors shown in the sample or pick your own, the color layout will make any palette look pulled together, and the final piece is sure to bring playful joy.

Finished Size

43 x 34in (109 x 86cm)

Yarn

Fingering weight (4ply) (#1 Superfine)

Shown here: Scheepjes Catona (100% mercerized cotton) 50g (137yd/125m); 2 balls each in following colors, unless otherwise specified:

- Yarn A: 205 Kiwi
- Yarn B: 403 Lemonade
- Yarn C: 385 Crystalline
- Yarn D: 524 Apricot
- Yarn E: 518 Marshmallow
- Yarn F: 413 Cherry
- Yarn G: 106 Snow White; 9 balls
- Yarn H: 505 Linen; 5 balls

Hook

- US size C/2 or D/3 (3mm) hook

Notions

- Stitch markers

Gauge (Tension)

20 dc x 10 rows = 4 x 4in (10 x 10cm) using a C/2 or D/3 (3mm) hook.

Pattern Notes

Three different motifs are made and joined using Whip-stitch Join (see General Techniques: Joining Methods) using Placement Guide for reference. A simple border is added to finish.

To join new yarns, slst in specified stitch.

Make Blanket Body

Motif 1 (make 12)

See Placement Guide for colors to use in each block.

SECTION 1 (LARGE 1-COLOR TRIANGLE)

Row 1 (RS): MR, beg dc, [ch1, 2dc-cl] 4 times, ch1, 1dc, turn. [4 2dc-cl, 2 dc, 5 ch1-sp]

Row 2: Beg dc, 3dc in next ch-sp, 5dc in each of next 3 ch-sp, 3dc in next ch-sp, 1dc, turn. [23 dc]

Row 3: Beg dc, ch1, dc3tog, [ch5, dc5tog] 3 times, ch5, dc3tog, ch1, 1dc, fasten off, do not turn. [3 dc5tog, 2 dc3tog, 2 dc, 4 ch5-sp, 2 ch1-sp]

Rejoin yarn in first st, ready to work another RS row.

Row 4 (RS): Beg dc in first st, [ch1, 8dc in next ch5-sp] 4 times, ch1, 1dc in final st, turn. [34 dc, 5 ch1-sp]

Row 5: 2sc in first ch-sp, [ch2, sk2, 1sc in next st/sp] 12 times, 1sc in same sp, turn. [15sc, 12 ch2-sp]

Row 6: Beg tr, ch1, 3tr in next st, *sk 1 ch-sp, 3dc in next ch-sp, 3sc in next ch-sp, 1sc in next sc, 3sc in next ch-sp, 3dc in next ch-sp; (3tr, ch3, 3tr) in next sc, rep from * once more, 3tr in next st, ch1, 1tr, turn. [14 tr, 12 dc, 14 sc, 2 ch1-sp, 1 ch3-sp]

Row 7: 2sc in next ch-sp, 19sc, 3sc in next ch-sp, 19sc, 2sc in next ch-sp, turn. [45 sc]

Row 8: Beg dc, ch1, 1dc in same st, [ch1, sk1, 1dc] 11 times, ch3, 1dc in same st, [ch1, sk1, 1dc] 11 times, ch1, 1dc in same st, turn. [26 dc, 25 ch1-sp]

Note: *Tr sts on Row 9 form tiny bobbles on RS.*

Row 9: (1sc, 1tr, 1sc) in first ch-sp, [1tr in next dc, 1sc in next ch-sp] 12 times, (1tr, 1sc) in same sp, [1tr in next dc, 1sc in next ch-sp] 12 times, (1tr, 1sc) in same sp, turn. [27 tr, 28 sc]

Row 10: Beg dc, ch1, *2dc in each of next 6 sc, (1dc, ch1, 1dc) in next sc, 2dc in each of next 6 sc; ch3, rep from * once more, ch1, 1dc in final st, turn. [54 dc, 5 ch1-sp]

Row 11: (Beg dc, ch1, 2dc) in first ch-sp, *[ch1, sk1, 1dc] 6 times, ch1, sk1, 1dc in ch-sp, [ch1, sk1, 1dc] 6 times; (2dc, ch3, 2dc) in next ch-sp, rep from * once more, ch1, (2dc, ch1, 1dc) in final ch-sp, turn. [36 dc, 30 ch1-sp, 1 ch3-sp]

Motif 1

Row 12: 4sc in next ch-sp, PM in first sc to mark cnr, 1sc in each st/sp to ch3-sp, 5sc in ch3-sp, 1sc in each st/sp to final ch-sp, 6sc in final ch-sp, PM in fourth sc to mark cnr, work across long edge as follows: [2sc in next dc, 2sc in next sc] twice, 3sc in next tr, 1sc in next sc, 2sc in each of next 4 dc, 2sc in center ring, PM in second st to mark center, 2sc in each of next 4 dc, 1sc in next sc, 3sc in next tr, [2sc in next sc, 2sc in next dc] twice, 2sc in next ch-sp, slst in first sc, fasten off, do not turn. [121 sc] Cont to Section 2.

SECTION 2 (SMALL STRIPED TRIANGLE)

Start with color shown for longest stripe and work up to shortest.

Row 1 (RS): Join Color 1 in marked center st, beg dc in same st, 20dc, dc3tog, turn. [22 sts]

Row 2: [3sc, bobble] to last 2 sts, 2sc, turn.

Row 3: Beg dc, 1dc in each st to last 3 sts, dc3tog, fasten off, do not turn. [2 sts dec]

Join Color 2 in first st, ready to work another RS row.

Row 4 (RS): Beg dc in first st, 1dc to last 3 sts, dc3tog, turn. [2 sts dec]

Rows 5 and 6: Rep Rows 2 and 3. [2 sts dec]

Motif 1 Chart

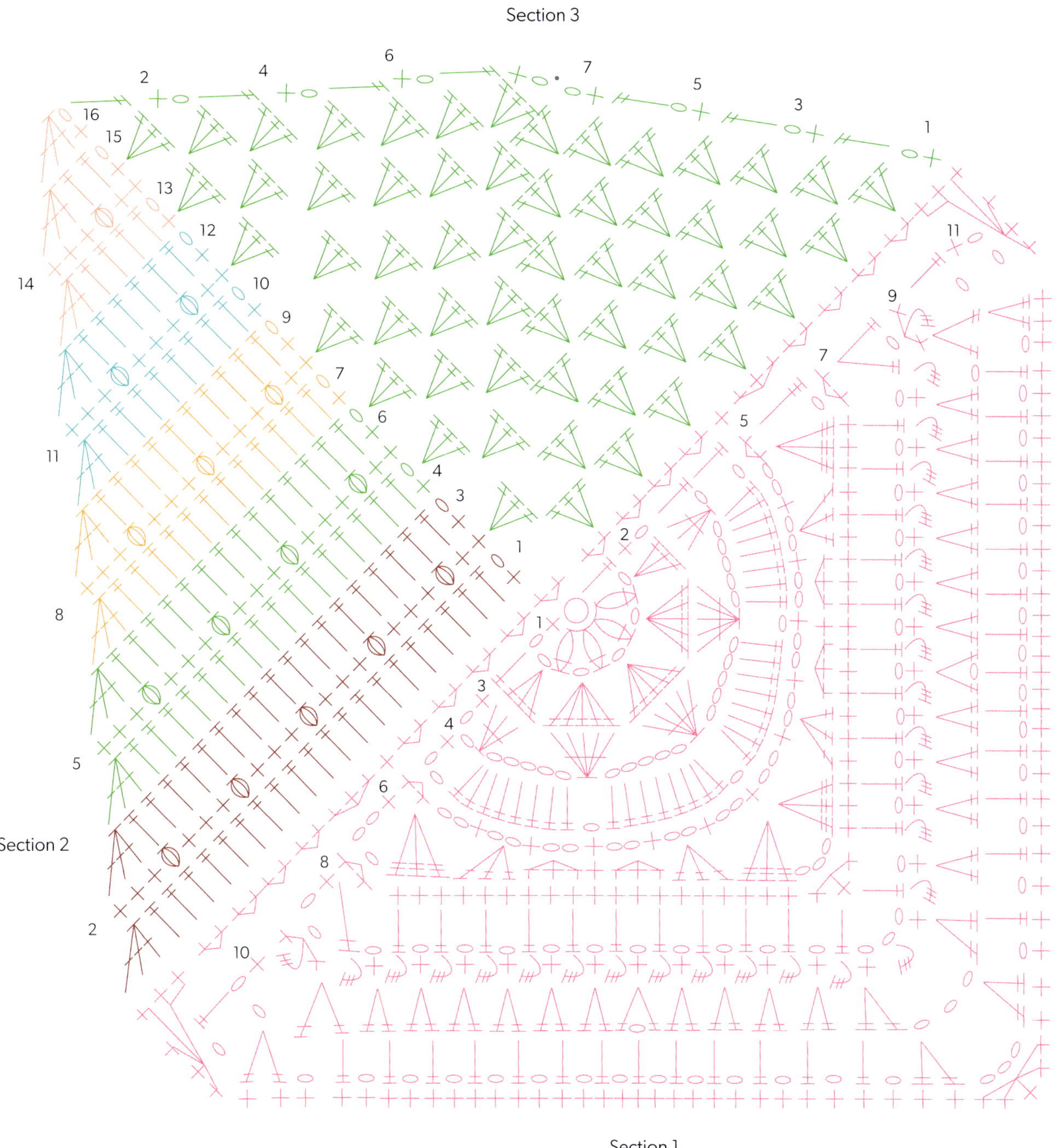

Rows 7–9: With Color 3, rep Rows 4–6. [1 dc3tog, 11 dc]

Rows 10–12: With Color 4, rep Rows 4–6. [1 dc3tog, 7 dc]

Rows 13–15: With Color 5, rep Rows 4–6 but do not fasten off after Row 15. [1 dc3tog, 3 dc]

Row 16: Beg dc, dc3tog, fasten off, turn. Cont to Section 3.

SECTION 3 (SMALL 1-COLOR TRIANGLE)

Row 1: With RS facing, join yarn in second marked cnr st, beg dc in same st, [sk2, 3dc in next st] 7 times, work across rows of Section 2 as follows: 3dc in sc from Row 2, 3dc in beg dc from Row 4, 3dc in beg dc from Row 6, 3dc in sc from Row 8, 3dc in sc from Row 11, 3dc in beg dc from Row 13, 3dc in beg dc from Row 15, 1dc in dc3tog, turn. [44 dc]

Row 2: Beg dc, [3dc between next 2 groups of 3 dc] 6 times, sk next 2 groups of 3 dc, [3dc between next 2 groups of 3 dc] 6 times, 1dc in final st, turn. [38 dc]

Row 3: Beg dc, [3dc between next 2 groups of 3 dc] to center 2 groups of 3 dc, sk center 2 groups of 3 dc, [3dc between next 2 groups of 3 dc] to last 4 dc, 1dc in final st, turn. [6 sts dec]

Rows 4–7: Rep Row 3 another 4 times. [8 dc]

Row 8: Beg dc in final st, fasten off, turn.

Half Border Row: Rejoin yarn in second marked cnr st, 2sc in same st, [2sc in next dc, 3sc in next dc] twice, 2sc in each of next 7 dc, [3sc in next dc, 2sc in next dc] twice, 3sc in dc3tog from Section 2, 3sc in next dc, 3sc in outer "leg" of each of next 9 dc3tog, 1sc in next sc, 3sc in next dc3tog as before, 2sc in first marked cnr st from Section 1, slst in same st, fasten off. [75 sc] Cont to Motif Border.

***Note:** All Motif borders are worked in Yarn G.*

Motif Border (RS): Join Yarn G in first sc of Half Border Row, 3sc in same st, [36sc, 3sc in next st] 4 times, omitting final 3sc on fourth rep, slst in first sc, fasten off and weave in ends. [156 sc]

Motif 2

Motif 2 (make 31)

BASE SQUARE

Rnd 1: With Yarn H, MR, beg tr, [3dc, 1tr] 3 times, 3dc, slst in beg tr. [4 tr, 12 dc]

Rnd 2: Beg tr in same st as slst, [2dc in same st, 3dc, (2dc, 1tr) in next st] 4 times, omitting final tr on fourth rep, slst in beg tr, fasten off, do not turn. [4 tr, 28 dc]

SECTION 1

Row 1 (RS): Join Yarn G in second st of Base Square, beg dc3tog across same and next 2 sts, 4dc, 5dc in next st, 4dc, dc3tog, turn. [2 dc3tog, 13 dc]

Row 2: [3sc, bobble] 3 times, 3sc, turn. [3 bobbles, 12 sc]

Row 3: Beg dc3tog, 4dc, 5dc in next st, 4dc, dc3tog, fasten off, do not turn. [2 dc3tog, 13 dc]

Row 4: (RS) With Yarn H, rep Row 3.

Row 5: Rep Row 2.

Row 6: Rep Row 3.

Rows 7–9: With Yarn G, rep Rows 4–6.

SECTION 2

Work as for Section 1, on opposite side of Base Square. Cont to Motif Border.

Motif Border (RS): Join Yarn G in final dc3tog of Section 1, 3sc in same st, [2sc in outer "leg" of same dc3tog, 3sc in each of next 5 dc3tog as before, 2sc in tr st of Base Square, 3sc in each of next 5 dc3tog as before, 2sc in next dc3tog as before, 3sc in top of same dc3tog, 6sc, 3sc in next st, 6sc, 3sc in next dc3tog] twice, omitting final 3sc on second rep, slst in first sc, fasten off and weave in ends. [114 sc]

Motif 3 (make 18)

Row 1 (RS): With Yarn G, MR, beg dc, 8dc, turn. [9 dc]

Row 2: (Beg dc, 1dc) in first st, 3dc, 5dc in next st, 3dc, 2dc in final st, turn. [15 dc]

Row 3: 2sc in first st, 6sc, 3sc in next st, 6sc, 2sc in final st, fasten off and weave in ends.

Join the Motifs

Lay motifs out using Placement Guide for position, and using Yarn G Whip-stitch Join motifs together to make blanket body (see General Techniques: Joining Methods).

Make Blanket Border

Rnd 1: Join Yarn G in top right cnr of blanket, [3sc in cnr, 12sc across long edge of each Motif 3 block, and 38sc across long edge of each Motif 2 block] 4 times, slst in first sc.

Rnd 2: Beg dc in cnr st, [4dc in same st, 1dc in each st to next cnr, 1dc in cnr st] 4 times, omitting final dc on fourth rep, fasten off and weave in ends.

Finishing

Weave in any rem ends and block blanket to given measurements and to flatten seams.

Placement Guide

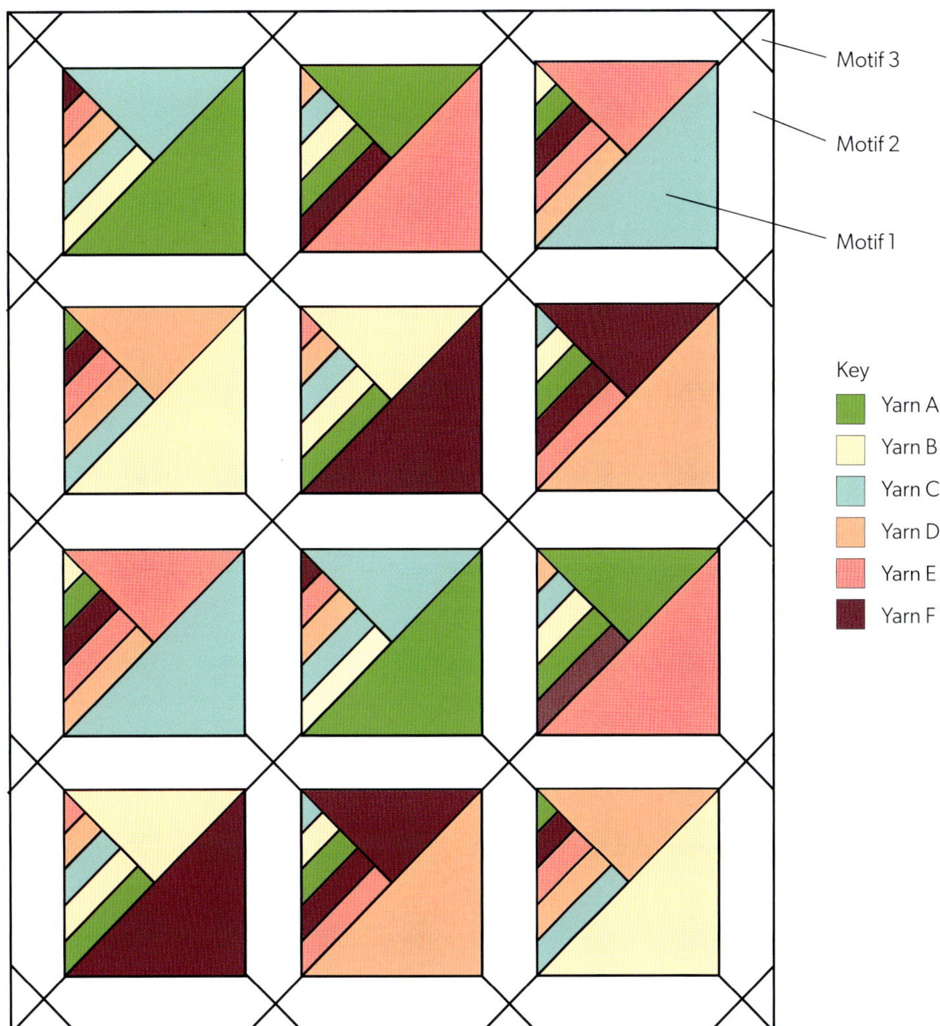

LITTLE BOAT BLANKET

Inspired by delightfully simple two-color quilt blocks, the Little Boat Blanket is the perfect modern classic. The geometric motifs are worked up individually and then joined as you go on the final round, for fast and easy construction. The linen stitch used is great for crafting in front of the television.

Finished Size

57 x 48in (145 x 122cm)

Yarn

Worsted (aran) weight (#4 Medium)

Shown here: Cascade 220 (100% Peruvian highland wool); 100g (220yd/200m); 1 hank in each of following colors, unless otherwise specified:

- Yarn A: White (8505); 5 hanks
- Yarn B: Paprika (9668)
- Yarn C: Jack O'Lantern (7824)
- Yarn D: Lemon Yellow (4147)
- Yarn E: Leaf Green (1002)
- Yarn F: Fern Heather (1035)
- Yarn G: Summer Sky Heather (9452)
- Yarn H: Cyan Blue (8891)

Hook

- US size G/6 (4mm) hook

Gauge (Tension)

13 dc x 7 rows = 4 x 4in (10 x 10cm) using a US G/6 (4mm) hook.

Pattern Notes

Before joining, motifs look similar on both sides. If desired, use a stitch marker to mark RS.

Each motif is made with Yarn A plus one contrasting color (CC).

Linen stitch uses reps of [ch1, 1sc in next ch-sp], so sc stitches are almost always worked in a ch-sp.

To join new yarns, slst in specified stitch.

Make Blanket Body

Motif 1 (make 4)

Use Yarn A plus 1 CC per motif in Yarn D, E, F, or H.

Row 1 (RS): With CC, MR, [1sc, ch1] twice, 1sc, turn. [3 sc, 2 ch-sp]

Row 2: (1sc, ch1, 1sc) in first ch-sp, ch1, (1sc, ch1, 1sc) in final ch-sp, turn. [4 sc, 3 ch1-sp]

Row 3: (1sc, ch1, 1sc) in first ch-sp, ch1, 1sc in next ch-sp, ch1, (1sc, ch1, 1sc) in final ch-sp, turn. [5 sc, 4 ch1-sp]

Row 4: (1sc, ch1, 1sc) in first ch-sp, [ch1, 1sc in next ch-sp] to final ch-sp, ch1, (1sc, ch1, 1sc) in final ch-sp, turn. [1 sc, 1 ch1-sp inc]

Rows 5–30: Rep Row 4 another 26 times. [32 sc, 31 ch1-sp]

Fasten off and weave in ends.

Row 31 (RS): Join Yarn A in first ch-sp, 1sc in same sp, [ch1, 1sc in next ch-sp] across to end, turn. [31 sc, 30 ch1-sp]

Rows 32–59: 1sc in first ch-sp, [ch1, 1sc in next ch-sp] to end, turn. [3 sc, 2 ch1-sp]

Row 60: 1sc in first ch-sp, ch1, 1sc in final ch-sp, turn.

Row 61: 1sc in ch-sp, fasten off and weave in ends.

Motif 2 (make 4)

Use Yarn A plus 1 CC per motif in Yarn C, D, E, or H.

Row 1 (WS): With CC, MR, [1sc, ch1] 3 times, 1sc, turn. [4 sc, 3 ch1-sp]

Row 2: (1sc, ch1, 1sc) in first ch-sp, [ch1, (1sc, ch1, 1sc) in next ch-sp] twice, turn. [6 sc, 5 ch1-sp]

Row 3: (1sc, ch1, 1sc) in first ch-sp, [ch1, 1sc in next ch-sp, ch1, (1sc, ch1, 1sc) in next ch-sp] twice, turn. [8 sc, 7 ch1-sp]

Row 4: (1sc, ch1, 1sc) in first ch-sp, [ch1, 1sc in next ch-sp] to center ch-sp, ch1, (1sc, ch1, 1sc) in center ch-sp, [ch1, 1sc in next ch-sp] to final ch-sp, ch1, (1sc, ch1, 1sc) in final ch-sp, turn. [2 sc, 2 ch1-sp inc]

Rows 5–15: Rep Row 4 another 11 times. [32 sc, 31 ch1-sp]

Fasten off and turn.

Motif 1

Motif 2

Row 16 (RS): Join Yarn A in first ch-sp, 1sc in same sp, [ch1, 1sc in next ch-sp] to center ch-sp, (1sc, ch1, 1sc) in center ch-sp, [ch1, 1sc in next ch-sp] to end.

Rows 17–30: Rep Row 16 another 14 times. [32 sc, 31 ch1-sp]

Fasten off and turn.

Row 31 (WS): Join CC in first ch-sp, 1sc in same sp, [ch1, 1sc in next ch-sp] to center ch-sp, ch1, 1sc in center ch-sp, turn. [16 sc, 15 ch1-sp]

On Rows 32–45 you will work across these sts only.

Rows 32–45: 1sc in first ch-sp, [ch1, 1sc in next ch-sp] to end, turn. [2 sc, 1 ch1-sp]

Row 46: 1sc in ch-sp, fasten off.

With WS facing, rejoin CC in center ch-sp and work as for Rows 31–46 to fill in second triangle. Fasten off and weave in ends.

Motif 3 (make 4)

Use Yarn A plus 1 CC per motif in Yarn B, F, G, or H.

Two triangles are worked with CC, then sides of triangles are worked across with Yarn A, and dec rows are worked until third triangle is made with Yarn A, then another Yarn A triangle is worked on opposing side, completing 4 triangles shown in Placement Guide.

TRIANGLES 1 AND 2 (MAKE 2)

With CC, work as for Rows 1–15 of Motif 2. [32 sc, 31 ch1-sp]

Fasten off and turn.

TRIANGLE 3

Row 1 (RS): Join Yarn A in first ch-sp of Row 15 on Triangle 1, 1sc in same sp, [ch1, 1sc in next ch-sp] 14 times, ch1, leave center ch-sp unworked, pick up Triangle 2, sk center ch-sp, 1sc in next ch-sp, [ch1, 1sc in next ch-sp] 14 times, working 14th sc in final ch-sp of Row 15 on Triangle 2, turn. [30 sc, 29 ch1-sp]

Motif 3

Row 2: 1sc in first ch-sp, [ch1, 1sc in next ch-sp] 13 times, sk center ch-sp, 1sc in next ch-sp, [ch1, 1sc in next ch-sp] 13 times, turn. [28 sc, 26 ch1-sp]

Rows 3–14: 1sc in first ch-sp, [ch1, 1sc in next ch-sp] to center 2 sc, sk2, 1sc in next ch-sp, [ch1, 1sc in next ch-sp] to end, turn. [4 sc, 2 ch1-sp]

Row 15: 1sc in each of next 2 ch-sp, fasten off.

TRIANGLE 4

Row 1 (RS): Rotate motif and join Yarn A in first ch-sp of Row 15 on rightmost triangle, 1sc in same sp, [ch1, 1sc in next ch-sp] 14 times, sk center ch-sp, 1sc in center ch-sp on Row 1 of Triangle 3 to close the gap, sk center ch-sp of Triangle 2, 1sc in next ch-sp, [ch1, 1sc in next ch-sp] 14 times working 14th sc in final ch-sp of Row 15 on Triangle 2, turn. [30 sc, 29 ch1-sp]

Rows 2–15: Work as for Triangle 3.

Fasten off and weave in ends.

Motif 4 (make 4)

Using Yarn A plus 1 CC per motif in Yarn B, C, F, or G.

CENTER PANEL

Rows 1–15: With CC, work as for Motif 1.

Fasten off.

Row 16 (RS): Join Yarn A in first ch-sp, [ch1, 1sc in next ch-sp] 15 times, turn. [15 sc, 15 ch1-sp]

Rows 17–45: [ch1, 1sc in next ch-sp] to end, turn. [15 sc, 15 ch1-sp]

Fasten off.

Row 46 (RS): Join CC in first sc, 1sc in same st, [ch1, 1sc in next ch-sp] to end, turn. [16 sc, 15 ch1-sp]

Rows 47–60: 1sc in first ch-sp, [ch1, 1sc in next ch-sp] to end, turn. [2 sc, 1 ch1-sp]

Row 61: 1sc in ch-sp, fasten off.

Create CC Triangle 3

Rotate motif to work across side of Yarn A square.

Row 1 (RS): Join CC in same ch-sp as final sc of Row 46, 1sc in same sp, ch1, 1sc in sc from next Yarn A row, [ch1, sk 1 Yarn A Row, 1sc in sc of next Yarn A row] 14 times, turn. [16 sc, 15 ch1-sp]

Rows 2–16: Work as for Rows 47–61 of Center Panel.

Fasten off.

TRIANGLE 4

Rotate motif to opposing side to add CC Triangle 4 as follows:

Row 1 (RS): Join CC in same ch-sp as attached Yarn A on Row 16, 1sc in same sp, ch1, 1sc in sc from next Yarn A row, [ch1, sk 1 Yarn A Row, 1sc in sc of next Yarn A row] 14 times, turn. [16 sc, 15 ch1-sp]

Rows 2–16: Work as for CC Triangle 3.

Fasten off and weave in ends.

Motif 4

Motif 5 (make 4)

Use Yarn A plus 1 CC per motif, using Yarn C, D, E, or G.

Row 1 (RS): With CC, ch47, 1sc in fourth ch from hook (turning ch counts as ch1), [ch1, sk 1 ch, 1sc] 21 times, turn. [22 sc, 22 ch1-sp]

Row 2: Join Yarn A in first sc, [ch1, 1sc in next ch-sp] 22 times, turn. [22 sc, 22 ch1-sp]

Rows 3–10: [ch1, 1sc in next ch-sp] 22 times.

Fasten off and turn.

Rows 11–20: Maintain pattern using Yarn A.

Rows 21–30: Maintain pattern using CC

Rows 31–41: Maintain pattern using Yarn A.

Fasten off and weave in ends

Motif 5

Join Motifs

Join motifs in numbered order and orientation in Placement Guide, adding 2 rounds to each motif and joining as you go on second round. First motif will be worked completely without joining, and subsequent motifs will be added on, joining on 1 or 2 sides.

MOTIF 1

Rnd 1 (RS): With CC used on motif, slst in top right cnr, [3sc in cnr, 30sc evenly across side] 4 times, slst in first sc. [134 sc]

Rnd 2: Beg dc in cnr sc, *ch1, 2dc in same st, [ch1, sk2, 2dc in next st] 11 times; rep from * 3 times more, omitting final dc on last rep, slst in beg dc, fasten off. [96 dc, 48 ch1-sp]

JOINING 1 SIDE: MOTIFS 2–4, 5, AND FIRST MOTIF IN EACH ROW BELOW

Rnd 1: Work as for Motif 1.

Rnd 2: Beg dc in cnr sc, ch1, 2dc in same st, [ch1, sk2, 2dc in next st] 11 times, slst in adjacent cnr sp on completed motif, 2dc in same st, [slst in adjacent ch-sp on completed motif, sk2, 2dc in next st] 11 times, slst in adjacent cnr sp, *2dc in same st, [ch1, sk2, 2dc in next st] 11 times; rep from * once more, omitting final dc, slst in beg dc, fasten off and weave in ends. [96 dc, 35 ch1-sp, 13 slst]

JOINING 2 SIDES: ALL OTHER MOTIFS

Rnd 1: Work as for Motif 1.

Rnd 2: Beg dc in cnr sc, ch1, 2dc in same st, [ch1, sk2, 2dc in next st] 11 times, slst in adjacent cnr sp on completed motif of row above, 2dc in same st, [slst in adjacent ch-sp on completed motif, sk2, 2dc in next st] 11 times, slst in adjacent cnr on completed motif of row above, and then on completed motif on the same row, 2dc in same st, [slst in adjacent ch-sp on completed motif, sk2, 2dc in next st] 11 times, slst in adjacent cnr sp on completed motif on the same row, ch1, 2dc in same st, [ch1, sk2, 2dc in next st] 11 times, omitting final dc, slst in beg dc, fasten off and weave in ends. [96 dc, 23 ch1-sp]

Make Blanket Border

Rnd 1 (RS): Join Yarn A in any cnr ch-sp, [3sc in cnr sp, 1sc in all sts and sps across to next cnr] 4 times, slst in first sc.

Rnd 2: [3sc in cnr st, 1sc in each st across to next cnr st] 4 times, slst in first sc, fasten off and weave in ends.

Finishing

Weave in any rem ends and block blanket to given measurements and to flatten seams.

Placement Guide

First join top row of motifs, then work down first column to join first motif in each row. Finally add remaining three motifs in each row in order.

HARMONY LOVE BLANKET

This blanket design was inspired by the colors of the rainbow, but it would look just as amazing in any color palette. The inclusion of a few diagonal rows of squares in a background color break up the design and add visual interest. This is the perfect project to take with you out and about, and you will love making the cute motifs.

Finished Size

70 x 63in (178 x 160cm)

Yarn

Worsted (aran) weight (#4 Medium)

Shown here: Knit Picks Heatherly Worsted (80% acrylic, 20% Merino wool) 100g (218yd/200m); 1 hank each in following colors, unless otherwise specified:

- Yarn A: Recess; 6 hanks
- Yarn B: Sweet Bing
- Yarn C: Peach Fuzz
- Yarn D: Butter
- Yarn E: Key Lime
- Yarn F: Cabana
- Yarn G: Lilac

Hook

- US size I/9 (5.5mm) hook

Gauge (Tension)

16 dc x 8 rows = 4 x 4in (10 x 10cm) using a US I/9 (5.5mm) hook.

Pattern Notes

Motifs are completed then joined with Slip-stitch Join through FLO with RS together (see General Techniques: Joining Methods).

To join new yarns, slst in specified stitch.

Make Blanket Body

Motifs (make 80)

Make 10 in each of Yarns B–G.

Make 20 in Yarn A; do not fasten off after Rnd 5 but cont to Rnd 6.

Rnd 1: MR, beg 4dc-cl [ch4, 4dc-cl] 3 times, ch4, 4dc-cl, slst in beg 4dc-cl. [4 4dc-cl, 4 ch4-sp]

Rnd 2: Beg dc in first ch-sp, [6dc in same ch-sp, ch1, 1dc in next ch-sp] 4 times, omitting final dc on fourth rep, slst in beg dc. [28 dc, 4 ch-sp]

Rnd 3: Beg 2dc-cl in next st, *[ch1, 2dc-cl] twice, ch1, 2dc-cl in same st, [ch1, 2dc-cl] twice, ch1, sk 2 dc, 2dc-cl; rep from * 3 times more, omitting final 2dc-cl on last rep, slst in beg 2dc-cl. [24 2dc-cl, 24 ch1-sp]

Rnd 4: [2sc in each of next 2 ch-sp, 3sc in next ch-sp, 2sc in each of next 2 ch-sp, 1sc in next ch-sp] 4 times, slst in first sc. [48 sc]

Motif

Motif Chart

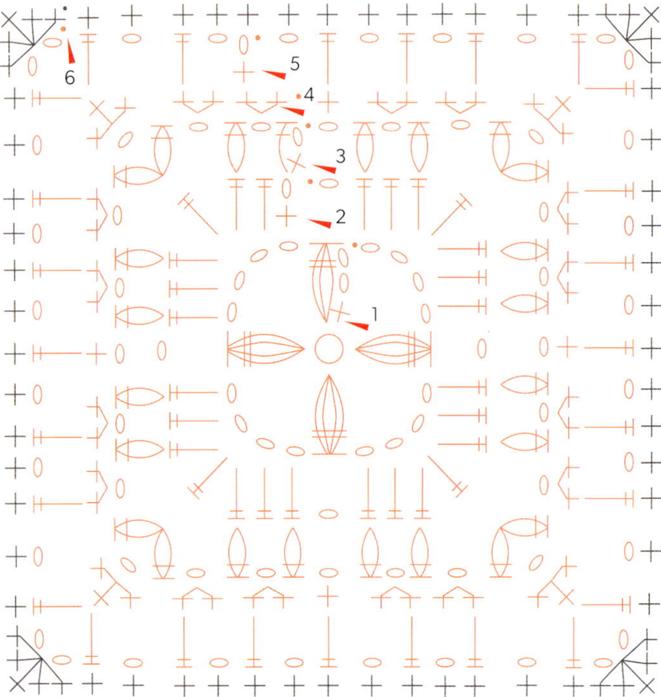

Rnd 5: Beg dc in next st, *[ch1, sk1, 1dc] twice, ch2, 1dc in same st, [ch1, sk1, 1dc] 4 times; rep from * 3 times more, omitting final dc on last rep, slst in beg dc, fasten off. [28 dc, 24 ch1-sp, 4 ch2-sp]

Rnd 6: Join Yarn A in any cnr sp, [5sc in cnr sp, 1sc in each st and ch-sp to next cnr] 4 times, slst in first sc, fasten off and weave in ends. [72 dc]

Join the Motifs

With Yarn G, and following Placement Guide for motif layout, Slip-stitch Join motifs together through both BLO with RS together, first joining seams horizontally and then rotating piece and joining seams vertically (see General Techniques: Joining Methods).

Make Blanket Border

Rnd 1: Join Yarn A to any cnr, *3sc in cnr, [13sc, sk next 2 cnr sts] 7 times, 13sc, 3sc in cnr, [13sc, sk next 2 cnr sts] 9 times, 13sc; rep from * once more, slst in first sc. [376 sts]

Rnd 2: *1sc in cnr st, ([ch3, 1sc] 3 times) in same st, [sk2 (1sc, ch3, 1sc) in next st] across to next cnr st; rep from * 3 times more, slst in first sc, fasten off and weave in ends.

Finishing

Weave in any rem ends and block blanket to given measurements and to flatten seams.

Placement Guide

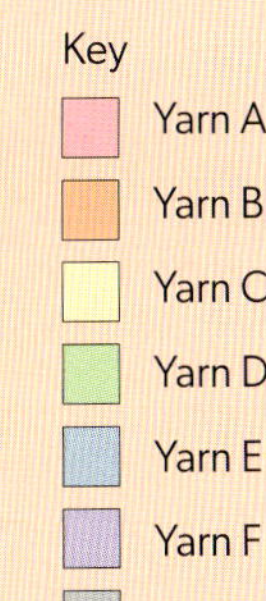

BOBBLE CHEVRON BLANKET

Created as a bookish spin on chevron quilt blocks, these motifs feature textured bobbles as a creative twist. The construction method is clever and simple while packing an opulent punch, which is accented by laying out the motifs in random orientations. Bobble Chevron has a classic and scholarly look that will perfectly decorate any room from a college dormitory to a cozy living room.

Finished Size

55 x 55in (139.5 x 139.5cm)

Yarn

Light worsted (DK) weight (#3 Light)

Shown here: Scheepjes Scrumptious (50% recycled polyester (recycled plastic bottles), 50% acrylic) 100g (328yd/300m); 1 ball each in following colors, unless otherwise specified:

- Yarn A: 307 Raspberry Mousse
- Yarn B: 312 Blackberry Honey Gelato
- Yarn C: 365 Summer Pudding
- Yarn D: 301 Charcoal Ice Cream
- Yarn E: 309 Strawberry Shortcake
- Yarn F: 314 Blue Glazed Doughnut
- Yarn G: 335 Raspberry Rock Candy
- Yarn H: 374 Blueberry Basil Galette
- Yarn I: 311 Chai Shortbread
- Yarn J: 323 Cinnamon Peach Cobbler
- Yarn K: 333 Poppy Seed Blondie
- Yarn L: 302 Buttercream Icing; 3 balls

Hooks

- US size E/4 (3.5mm) hook
- US size C/2 or D/3 (3mm) hook (for border)

Notions

Stitch markers

Gauge

19 dc x 10 rows = 4 x 4in (10 x 10cm) using a US E/4 (3.5mm) hook.

Pattern Notes

Motifs are worked up with MC yarn and two CC yarns foll Color Placement Guide, and then joined with Slip-stitch Join (see General Techniques: Joining Methods).

Working over yarn ends during first row of next section means faster finishing.

To join new yarns, slst in specified stitch.

Make Blanket Body

Motifs 1-49

See Motif Color Placement Guide for colors used.

Every section begins with RS facing, so after third row of each section, do not turn.

SECTION 1

Row 1 (RS): With MC, MR, beg dc, 8dc, turn. [9 dc]

Row 2: 2sc in first st, 1sc, bobble, 1sc, (1sc, bobble, 1sc) in next st, 1sc, bobble, 1sc, 2sc in final st, turn. [3 bobbles, 10sc]

Row 3: Beg dc, 2dc in same st, 5dc, 5dc in next bobble, 5dc, 3dc in final st, fasten off. [21 dc]

SECTION 2

Row 1 (RS): Join CC1 in first st, (beg dc, 2dc) in same st, 10dc, turn. [13 dc]

Row 2: 12sc, 2sc in final st, turn. [14 sc]

Row 3: Beg dc, 2dc in same st, 13dc, fasten off, PM in final dc. [16 dc]

SECTION 3

Note: *This section is worked across left edge, down Sections 1 and 2.*

Row 1: Join CC2 in top half of marked st, beg dc in same sp, 1dc in bottom half of same dc, 1dc in next sc, 1dc in top half of next dc, 1dc in bottom half of same dc, 1dc in center dc of Section 1, 9dc, 3dc in final st, turn. [18 dc]

Row 2: 2sc in first st, 17sc, turn. [19 sc]

Row 3: Beg dc, 17dc, 3dc in final st, fasten off, PM in beg dc. [21 dc]

SECTION 4

Row 1 (RS): Join MC in first st of Section 2, beg dc3tog over same and next 2 sts, 13dc, 5dc evenly across side edge of Section 3 ending in marked st, 4dc in same st, 19dc, 3dc in final st, turn. [1 dc3tog, 44 dc]

Row 2: 2sc in first st, [bobble, 2sc] 8 times, (bobble, 1sc) in same st, 1sc, [bobble, 2sc] 5 times, bobble, 1sc, sc2tog, turn. [1 sc2tog, 15 bobbles, 31 sc]

Row 3: Beg dc3tog, 17dc, 5dc in next st, 25dc, 3dc in final st, fasten off. [1 dc3tog, 50 dc]

Motif Color Placement Guide

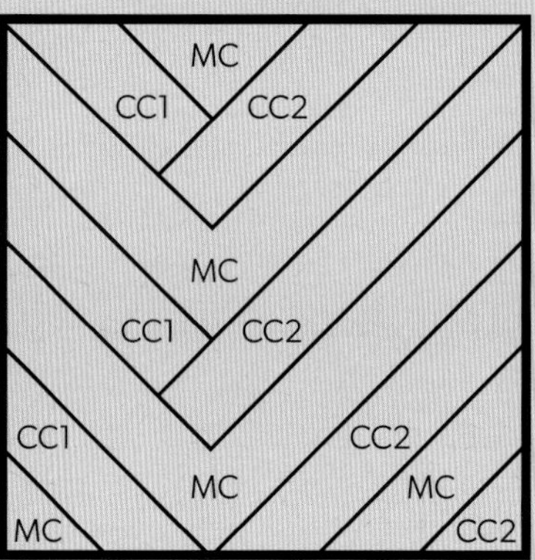

SECTION 5

Row 1 (RS): Join CC1 in beg dc3tog of Section 4, beg dc3tog over same and next 2 sts, 18 dc, turn.

Row 2: 17sc, sc2tog, turn.

Row 3: Beg dc3tog, 15 dc, fasten off, PM in final dc.

SECTION 6

Note: *This section is worked across left edge, down Sections 4 and 5.*

Row 1 (RS): Join CC2 in top half of marked st, beg dc in same sp, 4dc evenly across side edge of Section 5 as before, 1dc in center dc of Section 4, 27dc, dc3tog, turn. [1 dc3tog, 33 dc]

Row 2: Sc2tog, 32sc, turn.

Row 3: Beg dc, 29dc, dc3tog, fasten off, PM in beg dc. [1 dc3tog, 30 dc]

SECTION 7

Row 1 (RS): Join MC in first st of Section 5, beg dc3tog over same and next 2 sts, 13dc, 5dc evenly across side edge of Section 6 ending in marked st, 4dc in same st, 27dc, dc3tog, turn. [2 dc3tog, 49 dc]

Row 2: Sc2tog, [2sc, bobble] 9 times, 2sc, (bobble, 1sc) in same st, 1sc, [bobble, 2sc] 5 times, bobble, 1sc, sc2tog, turn. [2 sc2tog, 16 bobbles, 33 sc]

Row 3: Beg dc3tog, 17dc, 5dc in next st, 27dc, dc3tog, fasten off. [2 dc3tog, 49 dc]

SECTION 8

Row 1 (RS): Join CC1 in first dc3tog of Section 7, beg dc3tog over same and next 2 sts, 15 dc, dc3tog, turn.

Row 2: Sc2tog, 13sc, sc2tog, turn.

Row 3: Beg dc3tog, 9dc, dc3tog, fasten off.

SECTION 9

Row 1 (RS): Join CC2 in center dc of Section 7, beg dc3tog over same and next 2 sts, 25dc, dc3tog, turn.

Row 2: Sc2tog, 23sc, sc2tog, turn.

Row 3: Beg dc3tog, 19dc, dc3tog, fasten off.

SECTION 10

Row 1 (RS): Join MC in first st of Section 8, beg dc3tog over same and next 2 sts, 5dc, dc3tog, turn.

Row 2: Sc2tog, 1sc, bobble, 1sc, sc2tog, turn. [2 sc2tog, 1 bobble, 2 sc2tog]

Row 3: Beg dc5tog, fasten off.

Motif

Motif Color Sequence Table

Motif #	MC	CC1	CC2	Motif #	MC	CC1	CC2	Motif #	MC	CC1	CC2
1	C	G	A	18	I	H	F	35	A	G	E
2	K	G	L	19	D	G	K	36	K	G	C
3	I	G	J	20	C	A	G	37	F	K	H
4	F	G	J	21	E	F	H	38	L	G	I
5	K	G	D	22	I	G	J	39	A	H	C
6	A	H	E	23	B	D	H	40	F	I	G
7	C	L	G	24	I	D	G	41	A	L	H
8	I	G	K	25	E	H	L	42	J	C	H
9	D	E	H	26	A	H	K	43	B	L	G
10	B	G	J	27	K	G	F	44	J	B	H
11	E	G	D	28	L	C	H	45	C	G	B
12	J	G	B	29	J	H	F	46	J	G	E
13	L	G	E	30	A	G	L	47	B	H	L
14	I	G	D	31	B	H	E	48	F	D	G
15	L	G	C	32	D	G	J	49	I	L	G
16	A	B	G	33	B	G	F				
17	C	F	H	34	E	I	G				

SECTION 11

Row 1 (RS): Join MC in first st of Section 9, beg dc3tog, 15dc, dc3tog, turn.

Row 2: Sc2tog, [bobble, 2sc] 4 times, bobble, sc2tog, turn. [2 sc2tog, 5 bobbles, 8 sc]

Row 3: Beg dc3tog, 9dc, dc3tog, fasten off.

SECTION 12

Row 1 (RS): Join CC2 in first st of Section 11, beg dc3tog, 5dc, dc3tog, turn.

Row 2: Sc2tog, 3sc, sc2tog, turn.

Row 3: Beg dc5tog, fasten off. Cont to Motif Border.

Motif Border (RS): Join Yarn L in beg dc5tog from Row 3 of Section 12, 3sc in same st, *28sc evenly across side of motif as follows: [6sc across next section, 5sc across next section] twice, 6sc across next section ending just before next cnr, 3sc in cnr; rep from *3 times more, omitting final 3sc on last rep, slst in first sc, fasten off and weave in ends.

Join the Motifs

Lay motifs out in numbered order making 7 rows of 7 motifs, using Placement Direction Guide for orientation. With Yarn L, Slip-stitch Join motifs together through BLO with RS together (see General Techniques: Joining Methods). When all motifs are joined in rows in one direction, rotate the blanket 90 degrees and join rows until complete.

Make Blanket Border

Using smaller hook, join Yarn L in top right cnr of blanket, [3sc in cnr, sc in each st to next cnr] 4 times, slst in first sc, fasten off and weave in ends.

Finishing

Weave in any rem ends and block blanket to given measurements and to flatten seams.

Placement Direction Guide

1	2	3	4	5	6	7
8	9	10	11	12	13	14
15	16	17	18	19	20	21
22	23	24	25	26	27	28
29	30	31	32	33	34	35
36	37	38	39	40	41	42
43	44	45	46	47	48	49

SWEET TREAT BLANKET

The Sweet Treat Blanket was inspired by beautifully decorated, delicious-looking cookies and cakes. This pattern takes the fun aesthetic of frosted cookies and turns it into a bright, festive blanket design. For my demo blanket I used a Scheepjes yarn pack, but you can dive into your yarn stash and use yarn remnants to create something just as fun.

Finished Size

48 x 48in (122 x 122cm)

Yarn

Fingering (4ply) weight (#1 Superfine)

Shown here: Scheepjes Catona (100% mercerized cotton) 10g (27yd/25m) and 50g (137yd/125m):

- Yarn A: Snow White (106); 8 x 50g balls
- Yarn B: Jet Black (110); 2 x 50g balls
- CC yarns: Color pack includes 109 x 10g balls of complete Catona color range

Hooks

- US size C/2 or D/3 (3mm) hook

Gauge (Tension)

20 dc x 10 rows = 4 x 4in (10 x 10cm) using a US C/2 or D/3 (3mm) hook.

Pattern Notes

All motifs are worked separately then joined on an additional round as instructed in pattern.

The blanket is finished with one round of single crochet, and multicolor pompoms are added to points at top and bottom.

To keep track of motifs, refer to project image or stack hexagons by row.

To join new yarns, slst in specified stitch.

Make Blanket Body

Save all remnants from motifs to use to make colorful pompoms to add to blanket.

Flowers: 2dc in next st, turn and working in edge of each dc as if it were a ch-sp ([1sc, ch1, 2dc, ch1, 1sc] 3 times) in first dc, ([1sc, ch1, 2dc, ch1, 1sc] twice) in next dc, ch1, change to C1, turn.

Motif 1 Chart

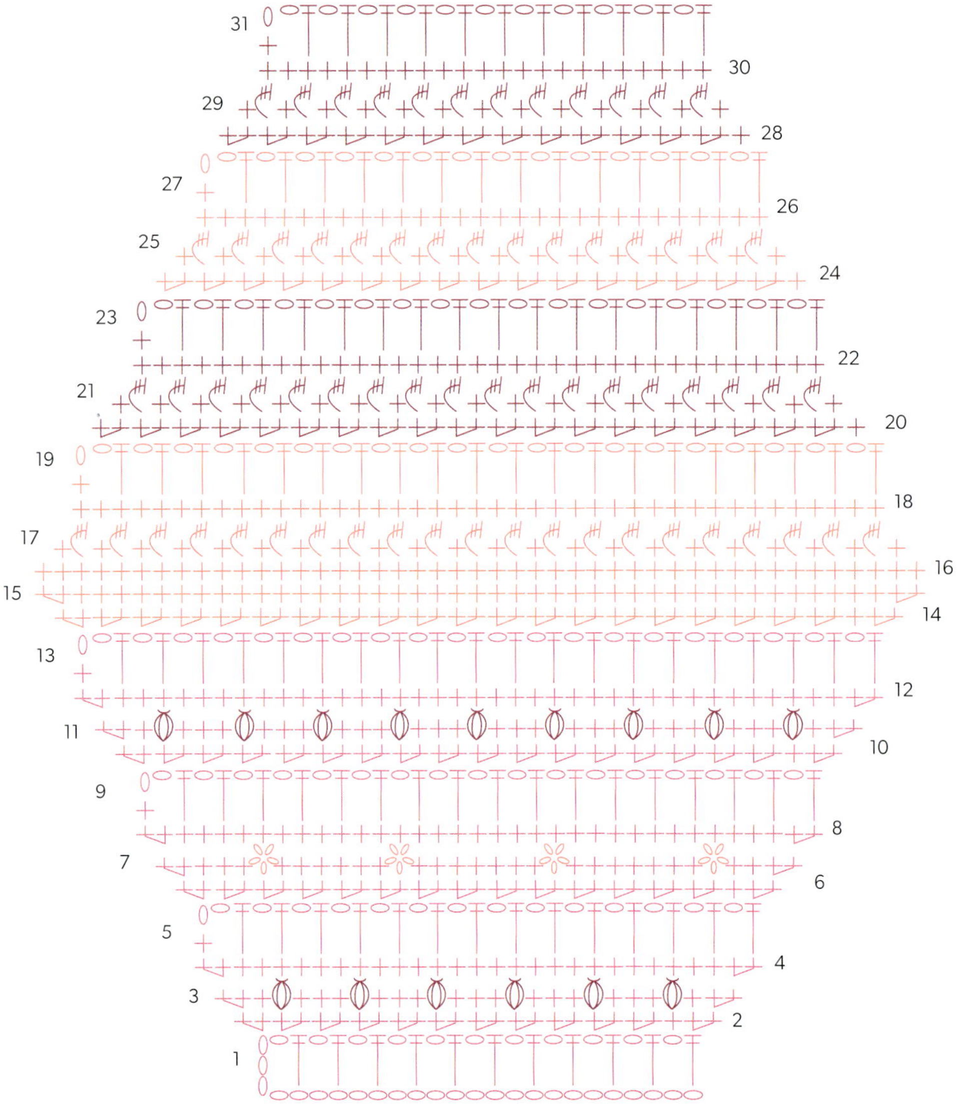

Flower Chart

Motif 1 (make 32)

Use C1, C2, and C3 as specified in Placement Guide.

Row 1 (WS): With C1, ch26, 1dc in sixth ch from hook, (skipped chs count as 1dc and ch1), [ch1, sk 1 ch, 1dc] 10 times, turn. [12 dc, 11 ch1-sp]

Row 2: 2sc in first st, 1sc in ch-sp, 2sc in each of next 10 ch-sp, 2sc in final st, turn. [25 sc]

Row 3: 2sc in first st, [1sc (change to C2 on final step), bobble (change to C1 on final step), 2sc] 6 times, 1sc in same st, fasten off C2, turn. [21 sc, 6 bobbles]

Row 4: With C1, 2sc in first st, 25sc, 2sc in final st, turn. [29 sc]

Row 5: Beg dc in first st, [ch1, sk1, 1dc] 14 times, turn. [15 dc, 14 ch1-sp]

Row 6: 2sc in first st, 1sc in ch-sp, 2sc in each of next 13 ch-sp, 2sc in final st, turn. [31 sc]

Row 7: 2sc in first st, 2sc (change to C3 on final step of second sc), make flower, [7sc (change to C3 on final step of last sc), make flower] 3 times, 3sc, 2sc in final st, fasten off C3, turn. [29 sc, 4 flowers]

Row 8: With C1, 2sc in first st, 31sc, 2sc in final st, turn. [35 sc]

Row 9: Beg dc in first st, [ch1, sk1, 1dc] 17 times, turn. [18 dc, 17 ch1-sp]

Row 10: 2sc in first st, 1sc in ch-sp, 2sc in each of next 16 ch-sp, 2sc in final st, turn. [37 sc]

Row 11: 2sc in first st, [1sc (change to C2 on final step), bobble (change to C1 on final step), 2sc] 9 times, 1sc in same st, fasten off C2, turn. [30 sc, 9 bobbles]

Row 12: With C1, 2sc in first st, 37sc, 2sc in final st, turn. [41 sc]

Row 13: Beg dc in first st, [ch1, sk1, 1dc] 20 times, turn. [21 dc, 20 ch1-sp]

Row 14: 2sc in first st, 1sc in ch-sp, 2sc in each of next 19 ch-sp, 2sc in final st, turn. [43 sc]

Row 15: 2sc in first st, 41sc, 2sc in final st, fasten off C1, turn. [45 sc]

Row 16: Join C3 in first st, 45sc, PM in first and final sts of this row to mark cnrs, turn.

***Note:** Tr sts on Rows 17, 21, 25 and 29 form tiny bobbles on RS.*

Motif 1

Row 17: 1sc in next st, [1tr, 1sc] until 1 st rem, turn. [2 sts dec]

Row 18: 1sc in first tr, 1sc in each st until 1 st rem, turn. [2 sts dec]

Row 19: Beg dc in first st, [ch1, sk1, 1dc] to end, turn. [Even sts, odd ch-sp]

Row 20: 1sc in first ch-sp, 2sc in each of rem ch-sp, fasten off C3, turn. [2 sts dec]

Join C2 in second st.

Rows 21–24: Rep Rows 17–20. [33 sc]

Join C3 in second st.

Rows 25–28: Rep Rows 17–20. [27 sc]

Join C2 in second st.

Rows 29–31: Rep Rows 17–19. [12 tr, 13 sc]

Motif Border Rnd: Cont with C2, 3sc in first dc, 1sc in next ch-sp, 2sc in each of next 10 ch-sp, 3sc in next st, 21sc evenly to marked st, 3sc in marked st, 21sc evenly to next cnr, (next 27 sts will be worked in Row 1 starting chs), 3sc in cnr ch, 21sc, 3sc in next cnr ch, 21sc evenly to next marked st, 3sc in marked st, 21sc evenly to beg, slst in first sc, fasten off and weave in ends.

Motif 2 (make 3)

Use C1, C2, and C3 as specified in Placement Guide.

Rows 1–15: Work as for Motif 1.

Row 16: With C1, work as for Motif 1, fasten off.

Note: *Motif Border Row is worked across 3 short sides.*

Motif Border Row: With RS facing, join C2 in final sc of Row 16, 2sc in same st, 21sc to next cnr ch, [3sc in cnr ch, 21sc] twice, 2sc in final cnr, fasten off and weave in ends.

Motif 3 (make 3)

Use C1, C2 and C3 as specified in Placement Guide.

Row 1 (RS): With C3, ch46, 1sc in second ch from hook, 44sc, turn. [45 sc]

Rows 2–16: Work as for Rows 17–31 of Motif 1.

Note: *Motif Border Row is worked across 3 short sides.*

Motif Border Row: With RS facing, join C2 in first sc of Row 1, 2sc in same st, 21sc to next cnr dc, 3sc in cnr st, 1sc in next ch-sp, 2sc in each of next 10 ch-sp, 3sc in next cnr dc, 21sc evenly to end of short side, 2sc in final st, fasten off and weave in ends.

Motif 4

Motif 4 (make 6)

Row 1 (RS): With Yarn B, ch23, 1dc in second ch from hook (skipped chs count as 1dc), 19dc, 2dc in final ch, turn. [23 dc]

Row 2: 23sc, turn.

Row 3: Beg dc, 1dc in same st, 21dc, 2dc in final st, fasten off, do not turn. [25 dc]

Join Yarn A to first st, ready to work another RS row.

Row 4 (RS): (Beg dc, 1dc) in first st, 23dc, 2dc in final st, turn. [2 sts inc]

Row 5: 1sc in each st to end, turn.

Row 6: (Beg dc, 1dc) in same st, 25dc, 2dc in final st, fasten off, do not turn. [2 sts inc]

Join Yarn B to first st, ready to work another RS row.

Rows 7–9: Rep Rows 4–6. [33 dc]

Join Yarn A to first st, ready to work another RS row.

Rows 10–12: Rep Rows 4–6. [37 dc]

Join Yarn B to first st, ready to work another RS row.

Row 13 (RS): Beg dc2tog, 35dc, dc2tog, turn. [2 sts dec]

Row 14: 1sc in each st to end, turn.

Row 15: Beg dc2tog, 1dc in each st to last 2 sts, dc2tog, fasten off, do not turn. [2 sts dec]

Join Yarn A to first st, ready to work another RS row.

Rows 16–18: Rep Rows 13–15. [29 sts]

Join Yarn B to first st, ready to work another RS row.

Rows 19–21: Rep Rows 13–15. [25 sts]

Join Yarn A to first st, ready to work another RS row.

Rows 22–24: Rep Rows 13–15. [21 sts]

Motif Border Rnd (RS): Slst in dc2tog, 3sc in same st, 21sc, 3sc in dc2tog, 21sc evenly to marked st, 3sc in marked st, 21sc to bottom edge of motif, 3sc in cnr ch, 21sc across chs, 3sc in cnr ch, 21sc evenly to next marked st, 21sc to beg, slst in first sc, fasten off and weave in all ends.

Motif 5 (make 2)

Rows 1–12: Work as for Motif 4.

Motif Border Row: With RS facing, using Yarn A, work as for Motif Border Row of Motif 2, fasten off and weave in ends.

Join the Motifs

MOTIFS 1 AND 4

Join all full hexagon motifs (1 and 4), following layout shown in Placement Guide.

Joining Rnd (first full hexagon motif): Join Yarn A in lower cnr of motif, beg dc in same st, *ch1, 2dc in same st, [ch1, sk3, 3dc in next st] 5 times, ch1, 2dc in cnr sc; rep from * 5 times more, omitting final dc on last rep, slst in beg dc, fasten off.

Joining Rnd (rem full hexagon motifs): Work as for first full hexagon motif, except on joining sides, instead of working single chains, slst in ch1-sp of corresponding adjacent motif side, making sure you are holding WS together.

Note: *Where a motif cnr comes to meet 2 joined motif cnrs, make 1 slst in cnrs of both motifs.*

MOTIFS 2, 3, AND 5

Join all half-hexagon motifs (2, 3, and 5), following layout shown in Placement Guide. Following instruction is how row will be worked in general, but on joining sides work in corresponding ch-sp of adjacent motif as before.

Joining Row (generic): Holding motif with long side at bottom edge, join MC1 in cnr sc, beg dc in same st, *ch1, 2dc in same st, [ch1, sk3, 3dc in next st] 5 times, ch1, 2dc in cnr sc; rep from * twice more, ch1, 1dc in same st, fasten off.

Cont to Blanket Border.

Placement Guide

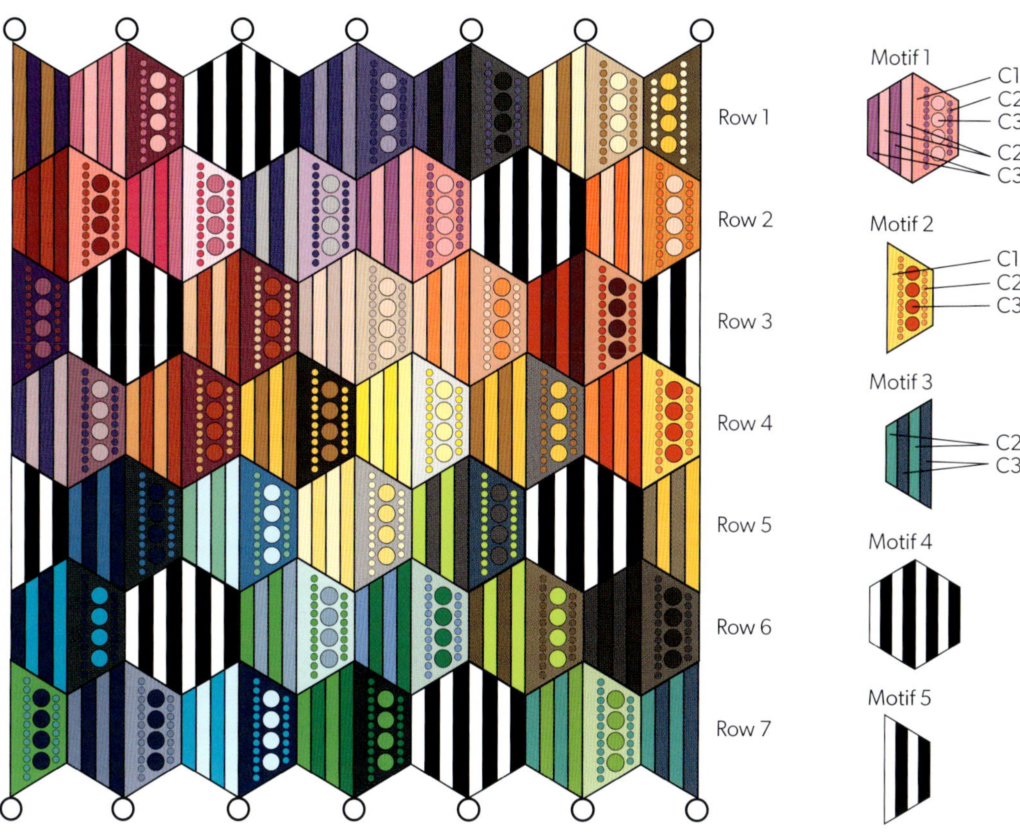

Make Blanket Border

Blanket Border Rnd: With MC1, slst in top right cnr ch-sp of blanket, *[3sc in cnr sp, 25sc, sc2tog across next 2 cnr ch-1 sp, 25sc] 6 times, 3sc in cnr ch-1 sp, [2sc across dc treating it as a ch-sp, 46sc across half-hexagon, 2sc across dc, 27sc across full hexagon] 3 times, 46sc across half-hexagon, 2sc across dc, rep from * once more, slst in first sc, fasten off and weave in ends.

Add Pompoms

Make 14 multicolor pompoms as follows: Divide colorful remnants into 14 piles. To make each pompom, wrap remnants (adding in MC1 to make pompom as full as it needs to be) around 4 fingers or a palm-width cardboard. Wrap a length of MC1 around middle of wrapped yarn and tie a tight and secure knot. Cut wrap loops across top and bottom edge, and fluff out to make pompom. Trim pompom until it is a nice sphere. Rep for rem 13 remnant piles to make 14 pompoms in total, making sure that all 14 are same size.

Stitch pompoms to seven points across top edge and bottom edge of blanket as shown in Placement Guide.

Finishing

Weave in any rem ends and block blanket to given measurements and to open up joined motif borders.

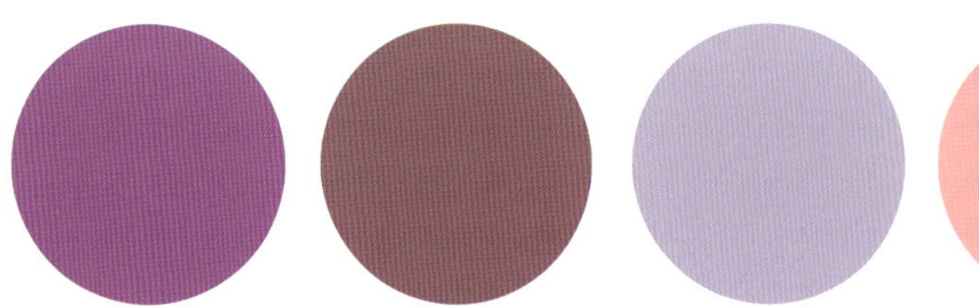

GEO PRISMA BLANKET

Sometimes I see a geometric pattern in the wild that I must make into a crochet blanket. This pattern was inspired by a stunning geometric rug I saw while furniture shopping. I loved how the hexagons and half hexagons combined with clever color placement to create a chaotic mix of surprising new shapes. You only need one shape to make the whole blanket – a half hexagon – so this piece packs maximum style for minimal effort.

Finished Size

47 x 43in (119.5 x 109cm)

Yarn

Light worsted (DK) weight (#3 Light)

Shown here: Scheepjes Colour Crafter (100% premium acrylic (anti-pilling) 100g (328yd/300m); 1 ball each in following colors, unless otherwise specified:

- Yarn A: 1010 Amsterdam
- Yarn B: 2016 Charleroi
- Yarn C: 2002 Gent
- Yarn D: 1084 Hengelo
- Yarn E: 1114 Eindhoven
- Yarn F: 1822 Delfzijl; 2 balls
- Yarn G: 1002 Ede; 2 balls
- Yarn H: 1001 Weert; 3 balls

Hook

- US size G/6 (4mm) hook

Notions

- Stitch markers
- Tapestry needle

Gauge (Tension)

20 dc x 10 rows = 4 x 4in (10 x 10cm) using a US G/6 (4mm) hook.

Pattern Notes

Three same size motifs are made in different ways to add a textural element.

Half-hexagon motifs are joined with Whip-stitch Join to make full hexagons, which are joined with Slip-stitch Join to make blanket (see General Techniques: Joining Methods).

To join new yarns, slst in specified stitch.

Make Blanket Body

Motif 1

Row 1 (WS): MR, beg dc, [ch1, 2dc] 3 times, ch1, 1dc, turn. [8 dc, 4 ch1-sp]

Row 2: Beg dc in first ch-sp, ch1, 2dc in same sp, (2dc, ch1, 2dc) in each of next 2 ch-sp, (2dc, ch1, 1dc) in final ch-sp, turn. [14 dc, 4 ch1-sp]

Row 3: Beg dc in first ch-sp, [ch1, 1dc in same sp, 1dc in each st to next ch-sp, 1dc in next ch-sp] 3 times, ch1, 1dc in same sp, turn. [6 dc inc]

Rows 4–7: Rep Row 3. [44 dc, 4 ch1-sp]

Row 8: 2sc in first ch-sp, [14sc, 3sc in next ch-sp] 3 times, omitting final sc on third rep, fasten off leaving arm's length tail to join later. [55sc]

Motif 2

Rows 1 and 2: Work as for Rows 1 and 2 of Motif 1.

Row 3: Beg dc in first ch-sp, [ch1, 2dc in same ch-sp, 2dc between next 2 groups of 2 dc, 2dc in next ch-sp] 3 times, ch1, 1dc in same sp, turn. [20 dc, 4 ch2-sp]

Row 4: Beg dc in first ch-sp, *ch1, 2dc in same sp, [2dc between next 2 groups of 2 dc] twice, 2dc in next ch-sp; rep from * twice more, ch1, 1dc in same sp, turn. [26 dc, 4 ch1-sp]

Row 5: Beg dc in first ch-sp, *ch1, 2dc in same sp, [2dc between next 2 groups of 2 dc] 3 times, 2dc in next ch-sp; rep from * twice more, ch1, 1dc in same sp, turn. [32 dc, 4 ch1-sp]

Row 6: Beg dc in first ch-sp, *ch1, 2dc in same sp, [2dc between next 2 groups of 2 dc] 4 times, 2dc in next ch-sp; rep from * twice more, ch1, 1dc in same ch-sp, turn. [38 dc, 4 ch1-sp]

Row 7: Beg dc in first ch-sp, *ch1, 2dc in same ch-sp, [2dc between next 2 groups of 2 dc] twice, 3dc between next 2 groups of 2 dc, [2dc between next 2 groups of 2 dc] twice, 2dc in next ch-sp; rep from * twice more, ch1, 1dc in same ch-sp, turn. [47 dc, 4 ch1-sp]

Row 8: 2sc in first ch-sp, [15sc, 3sc in next ch-sp] 3 times, omitting final sc on third rep, fasten off leaving arm's length tail to join later. [55sc]

Motif Color Amount Table

Yarn Color	Motif 1	Motif 2	Motif 3
A	3	4	3
B	3	3	3
C	3	4	3
D	4	3	4
E	3	3	3
F	3	3	3
G	5	5	5
H	8	8	9

Make number of each motif in colors as shown in Motif Color Amount Table.

Motif 1

Motif 3

Rows 1 and 2: Work as for Rows 1 and 2 of Motif 1.

Row 3: Beg dc in first ch-sp, *ch1, 1dc in same sp, [ch1, sk1, 1dc] twice, ch1, 1dc, ch1, 1dc in next ch-sp; rep from * twice more, ch1, 1dc in same sp, turn. [14 dc, 13 ch1-sp]

Row 4: (Beg dc, ch1, 1dc) in first ch-sp, [1dc in each st/sp to next cnr ch-sp, (1dc, ch1, 1dc) in cnr ch-sp] twice, ch1, 1dc in each st/sp to last ch-sp, (1dc, ch1, 1dc) in final ch-sp, turn. [15 dc inc, 9 ch1-sp dec]

Row 5: (Beg dc, ch1, dc) in first ch-sp, *[ch1, sk1, 1dc] to 1 st before next ch-sp, ch1, (1dc, ch1, 1dc) in ch-sp; rep from * twice more, turn. [9 dc dec, 15 ch1-sp inc]

Rows 6–7: Rep Rows 4 and 5. [26 dc, 25 ch1-sp]

Row 8: 2sc in first ch-sp, *[1sc in next st, 1sc in next ch-sp] 7 times, 1sc in next st, 3sc in next ch-sp; rep from * twice more, omitting final sc on third rep, fasten off leaving arm's length tail to join later. [55 sc]

Join the Motifs

Refer to Placement Guide for motif type, color, and orientation as you join pieces together.

CREATE FULL HEXAGONS

Pair hexagons, paying attention to motif number and yarn color. Holding motifs with RS together, join motifs along long edge using Slip-stitch Join (see General Techniques: Joining Methods), working into stitches rather than loops. Yarn tail of either color motif can be used to join. Eight motifs will be left over to fill gaps at top and bottom edges.

JOIN FULL HEXAGONS TO MAKE BLANKET BODY

Refer to Placement Guide for motif type, color, and orientation as you join pieces together.

Using yarn tails where possible and joining new yarn with slst where needed, follow Placement Chart and use Whip-stitch Join (see General Techniques: Joining Methods) to join full hexagons through BLO, paying attention to orientation of motifs.

Placement Guide

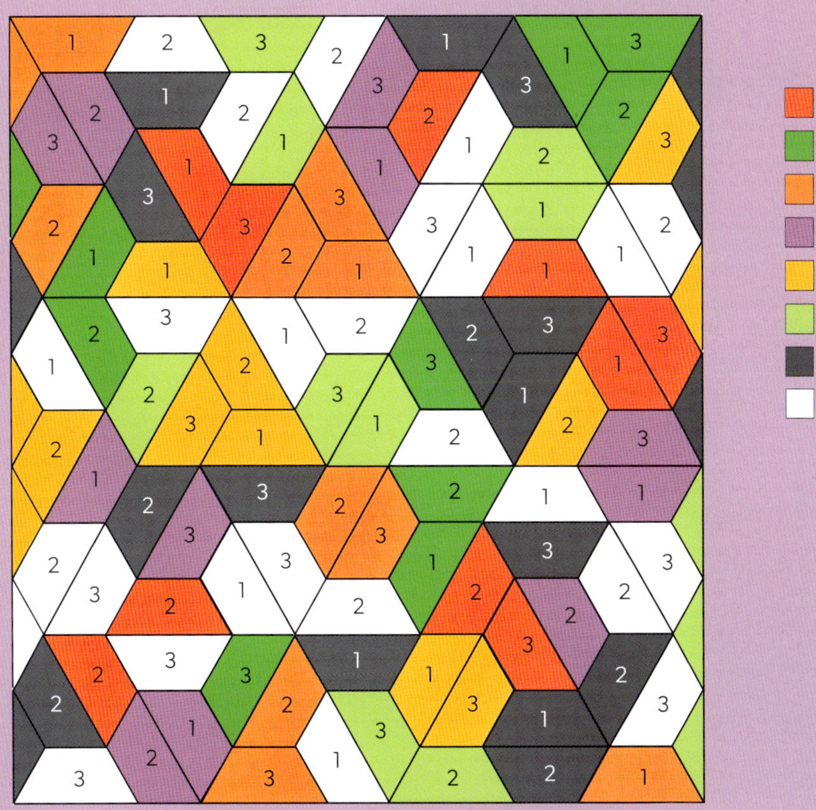

Squaring the Edges

ADD HALF HEXAGONS

Using same method, add 4 motifs at top edge, and 4 motifs at bottom edge to complete Blanket Body. Cont to Fill Triangle.

FILL TRIANGLE

All 7 triangle gaps down each long side of blanket are filled separately.

Row 1: Join Yarn B in second st of Row 8 on top left motif of blanket, 1sc in same st, 17sc, 1sc in cnr of next motif, 17sc ending in st just before next cnr sc, turn. [36 sc]

Row 2: Slst in first 2 sts, 2sc, 2hdc, 11dc, sk2, 11dc, 2hdc, 2sc, turn, leaving final 2 sc unworked. [22 dc, 4 hdc, 4 sc]

Row 3: Slst in first 2 sts, 2sc, 2hdc, 8dc, sk2, 8dc, 2hdc, 2sc, turn. [16 dc, 4 hdc, 4 sc]

Row 4: Slst in first 2 sts, 2sc, 2hdc, 5dc, sk2, 5dc, 2hdc, 2sc, turn. [10 dc, 4 hdc, 4 sc]

Row 5: Slst in first 6 sts, 2sc, sk2, 2sc, fasten off and weave in ends.

With colors shown in Placement Guide, fill rem 13 triangle gaps in this manner. Cont to Blanket Border.

Fill Triangle

Make Blanket Border

Rnd 1 (RS): Join Yarn H in first st of Row 8 on top left motif of blanket, 3sc in same st, *[28sc across fill triangle, 1sc in cnr st of hexagon motif] 6 times, 28sc across final fill triangle of this side, 3sc in final sc of Row 8 on bottom left motif of blanket, [31sc across long edge of half-hexagon, 19sc across full hexagon] 3 times, 31sc across final half-hexagon, 3sc in first st of Row 8 of bottom right motif on blanket; rep from * once more, omitting final 3sc, slst in first sc.

Rnd 2: [3sc in cnr st, 1sc in each st to next cnr] 4 times, slst in first sc.

Rnd 3: Beg dc in cnr st, *ch1, 1dc in same st, [ch1, sk1, 1dc] across, ending in next cnr st; rep from * 3 times, omitting final dc on last rep, slst in beg dc.

Rnd 4: [3sc in cnr ch-sp, 1sc in each st/sp to next cnr sp] 4 times, slst in first sc, fasten off and weave in ends.

Finishing

Weave in any rem ends and block blanket to given measurements and to flatten seams.

GRAND MOSAIC BLANKET

Picture yourself admiring this blanket on your lap as a true work of art! The mesmerizing color and design, outlined in crisp white, make for a smart and artful piece, and while the motifs may seem complicated, the clever pattern writing makes it simpler to make than it looks. You can enjoy this cozy blanket in front of the television or relaxing in bed, and it is sure to make you feel happy.

Finished Size

45 x 45in (114.5 x 114.5cm)

Yarn

Sport (4ply) weight (#2 Fine)

Shown here: Scheepjes River Washed (78% cotton, 22% acrylic) 50g (142yd/130m), in following colors:

- Yarn A: 962 Narmada; 2 balls
- Yarn B: 955 Po; 2 balls
- Yarn C: 941 Colorado; 2 balls
- Yarn D: 952 Rhine; 1 ball
- Yarn E: 961 Mersey; 4 balls
- Yarn F: 956 Avon; 3 balls
- Yarn G: 942 Steenbras; 3 balls
- Yarn H: 959 Ural; 2 balls

Scheepjes Stone Washed (78% cotton, 22% acrylic), 50g (142yd/130m) in following color:

- Yarn I: 801 Moon Stone; 3 balls

Hook

- US size E/4 (3.5mm) hook

Notions

Stitch markers

Gauge (Tension)

20 dc x 10 rows = 4 x 4in (10 x 10cm) using a US E/4 (3.5mm) hook.

Pattern Notes

Motifs are completed then joined with Slip-stitch Join (see General Techniques: Joining Methods), which creates a neat, crisp frame.

Placement Guide shows joining order.

To join new yarns, slst in specified stitch.

Make Blanket Body

Motif 1 (make 4)

CENTER MEDALLION (MAKE 1)

Rnd 1 (RS): With Yarn A, MR, beg 2dc-cl, [ch1, 2dc-cl] 7 times, ch1, slst in beg 2dc-cl. [8 2dc-cl, 8 ch1-sp]

Rnd 2: Beg 2dc-cl in first ch-sp, [ch1, 2dc-cl in same sp, ch1, 2dc-cl in next ch-sp] 8 times, omitting final ch1 and 2dc-cl on eighth rep, 1sc in beg 2dc-cl (counts as final ch-1 sp). [16 2dc-cl, 16 ch1-sp]

Rnd 3: 1sc in final ch1-sp, [ch3, pc in next ch-sp, ch3, 1sc in next ch-sp] 8 times, omitting final sc on eighth rep, slst in first sc, fasten off, PM in scs. [8 pc, 8 sc, 16 ch3-sp]

Rnd 4: Join Yarn B, [(1sc, 1hdc, 1dc, 1tr) in next ch-sp, ch1, (1tr, 1dc, 1hdc, 1sc) in next ch-sp] 8 times, slst in first sc, fasten off. [16 tr, 16 dc, 16 hdc, 16 sc, 8 ch1-sp]

Rnd 5: Join Yarn C in next st, 1sc in same st, [2sc, ch2, (2dc-cl, ch2, 2dc-cl) in next ch-sp, ch2, 3sc, sk1, FP2tr-cl around marked sc from Rnd 3, sk1, 1sc] 8 times omitting final sc on eighth rep, slst in first sc, fasten off. [8 FP2tr-cl, 16 2dc-cl, 48 sc, 24 ch2-sp]

Rnd 6: Join Yarn D in second ch-sp, [ch3, (3tr-cl, ch3, 3tr-cl) in FP2tr-cl, ch3, sk 1 ch-sp, slst in next ch-sp] 8 times, omitting final slst on eighth rep, slst in first slst, fasten off. [16 3tr-cl, 8 slst, 24 ch3-sp]

Rnd 7: Join Yarn B in first ch-sp, 1sc in same sp, [(4tr, ch3, 4tr) in next ch-sp, 1sc in next ch-sp, ch1, pc in ch3-sp from Rnd 5 and around slst from Rnd 6 together, ch1, 1sc in next ch-sp] 8 times, omitting final sc on eighth rep, slst in first sc, fasten off. [8 pc, 64 tr, 16 sc, 16 ch1-sp, 8 ch3-sp]

Rnd 8: Join Yarn H in any ch3-sp, 3sc in same sp, [3sc, 1hdc, 1dc in sc, 1dc in next sc, 1hdc, 3sc, 3sc in next ch-sp] 8 times, omitting final 3sc on eighth rep, slst in first sc, fasten off and weave in ends. PM in first st. [16 dc, 16 hdc, 72 sc]

Motif 1 Center Medallion

Center Medallion Chart

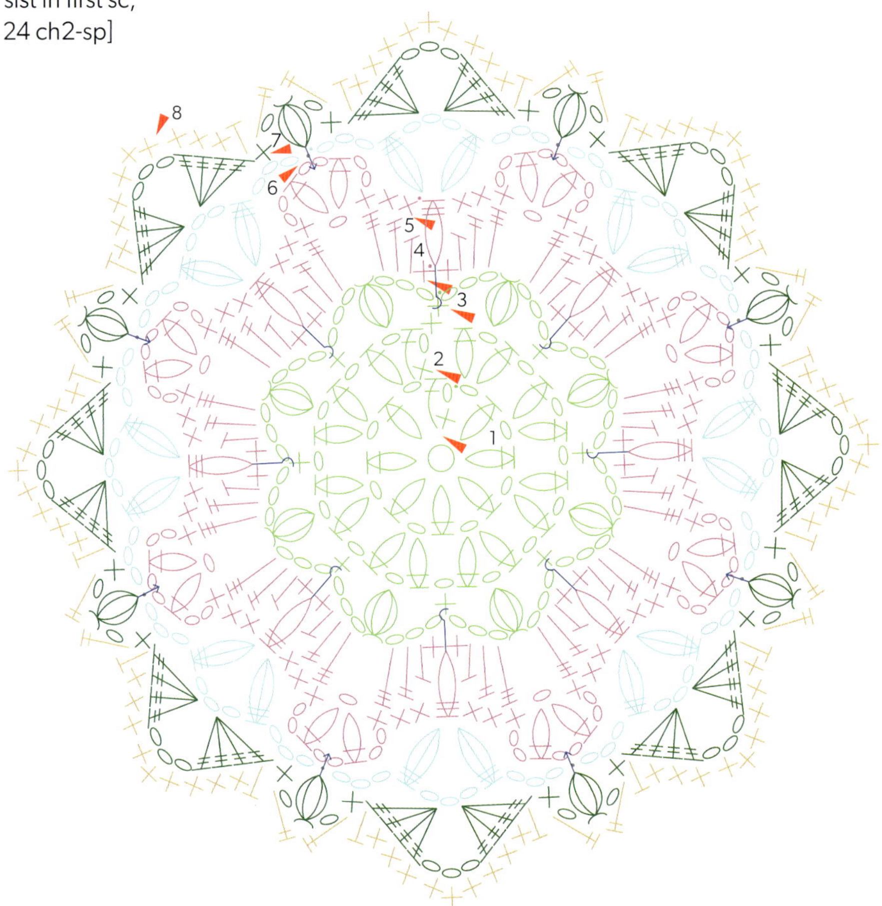

OUTER MEDALLIONS (MAKE 8)

Outer Medallions (OM) are joined to Center Medallion and each other on final round using PLT Join (see General Techniques: Joining Methods).

Rnd 1 (RS): With Yarn E, MR, beg 2dc-cl, [ch2, 2dc-cl] 5 times, ch2, slst in beg 2dc-cl. [6 2dc-cl, 6 ch2-sp]

Rnd 2: Beg 2dc-cl in first ch-sp, [ch1, 2dc-cl in same ch-sp, ch1, 2dc-cl in next ch-sp] 6 times, omitting final 2dc-cl on sixth rep, slst in beg 2dc-cl, fasten off. [12 2dc-cl, 12 ch1-sp]

Rnd 3: Join Yarn F in second ch-sp, 1sc in same sp, [ch3, pc in next ch-sp, ch3, 1sc in next ch-sp] 6 times, omitting final sc on sixth rep, slst in first sc, fasten off. [6 pc, 6 sc, 12 ch3-sp]

Rnd 4: Join Yarn G in any ch-sp, 1sc in same sp, [ch3, 1sc in next ch-sp] 11 times, ch3, slst in first sc. [12 sc, 12 ch3-sp]

Rnd 5: [3sc in next ch-sp, 2sc in next sc] 12 times, slst in first sc. [60 sc]

Rnd 6: 60sc, slst in first sc, fasten off.

Join Yarn H in next st and work Rnd 7 for OM you are working.

Rnd 7 (OM 1): 1sc in same st, 40sc, PLT in marked st on Center Medallion, [1sc, PLT] 10 times, 9sc, slst in first sc, fasten off. Mark 37th st for joining OM 8 later on. [60 sc] Cont to Motif Border.

Rnd 7 (OM 2–7): 1sc in same st, 32sc, PLT in final st of prev OM, [1sc, PLT] 4 times, 4sc, PLT to Center Medallion as for OM 1, [1sc, PLT] 10 times, 9sc, slst in first sc, fasten off. [60 sc] Cont to Motif Border.

Rnd 7 (OM 8): 1sc in same st, 32sc, PLT in final st of prev OM, [1sc, PLT] 4 times, 4sc, PLT to Center Medallion as for OM 1, [1sc, PLT] 10 times, 4sc, PLT in marked st on OM 1, [1sc, PLT] 4 times, 1sc, slst in first sc, fasten off and weave in ends. [60 sc] Cont to Motif Border.

MOTIF BORDER

Rnd 1: Join Yarn A in third sc of any OM, beg dc in same st, *3dc, [3dc in next st, 1dc, 1hdc, 4sc, 1hdc, 1dc] twice, 3dc in next st, 4dc, 1dc in third st on next OM; rep from * 7 times more, omitting final dc on last rep, slst in beg dc, fasten off. [168 dc, 32 hdc, 64 sc]

Rnd 2: Join Yarn I in sixth dc of Rnd 1, 1sc in same st, [10sc, 3sc in next st, 11sc, 1hdc, 1dc, 1tr, ch1, sk4, 1tr, 1dc, 1hdc, 1sc] 8 times, omitting final sc on eighth rep, slst in first sc, fasten off and weave in ends. [16 tr, 16 dc, 16 hdc, 200 sc, 8 ch1-sp]

Outer Medallion Chart

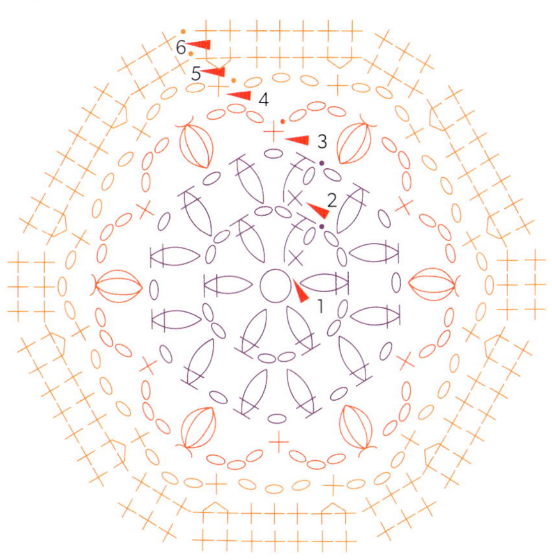

Motif 1 Joining

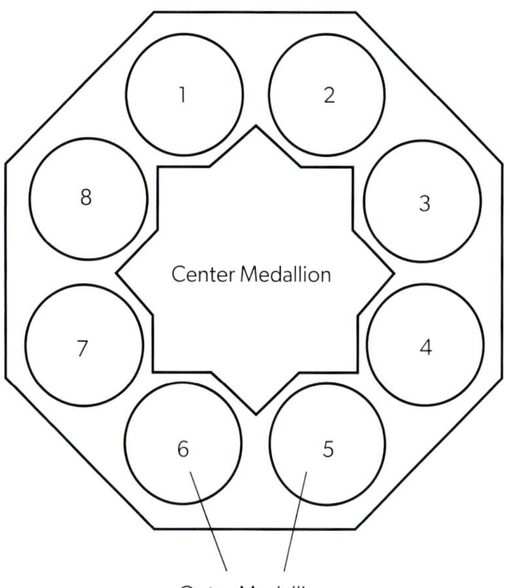

Motif 2 (make 8)

CENTER MEDALLION (MAKE 1)

Rows 4, 5, 6, 7, and 8 are all worked as RS rows. Join yarn where instructed with RS facing.

Row 1 (RS): With Yarn A, MR, beg dc, [ch1, 2dc-cl] 3 times, ch1, 1dc, turn. [3 2dc-cl, 2 dc, 4 ch1-sp]

Row 2: Beg dc, [ch1, 2dc-cl] twice in each of next 4 ch-sp, ch1, 1dc in final st, turn. [8 2dc-cl, 2 dc, 9 ch1-sp]

Row 3: 1sc in first ch-sp, [ch4, pc in next ch-sp, ch4, 1sc in next ch-sp] 4 times, fasten off, PM in scs, do not turn. [4 pc, 5 sc, 8 ch4-sp]

Row 4 (RS): Join Yarn B in first st, [(1sc, 1hdc, 1dc, 1tr) in next ch-sp, ch1, (1tr, 1dc, 1hdc, 1sc) in next ch-sp] 4 times, fasten off, do not turn. [8 tr, 8 dc, 8 hdc, 8 sc, 4 ch1-sp]

Row 5 (RS): Join Yarn C in first marked sc from Row 3, (FPsc, ch2, FPtr) around same st (counts as 1 FP2tr-cl), [3sc, ch2, (2dc-cl, ch2, 2dc-cl) in ch-sp, ch2, 3sc, FP2tr-cl around marked sc from Rnd 3, sk2] 4 times, omitting final sk2 on fourth rep, fasten off, do not turn. [5 FP2tr-cl, 8 2dc-cl, 24 sc, 12 ch2-sp]

Row 6 (RS): Join Yarn D in first FP2tr-cl, beg tr in same st, ch1, [3tr-cl in same st, ch3, sk 1 ch-sp, slst in next ch-sp, ch3, 3tr-cl in next FP2tr-cl, ch3] 4 times, making ch1 instead of final ch3 on fourth rep, 1tr in same st, fasten off, do not turn. [8 3tr-cl, 2 tr, 4 slst, 11 ch3-sp, 2 ch1-sp]

Motif 2 Joining

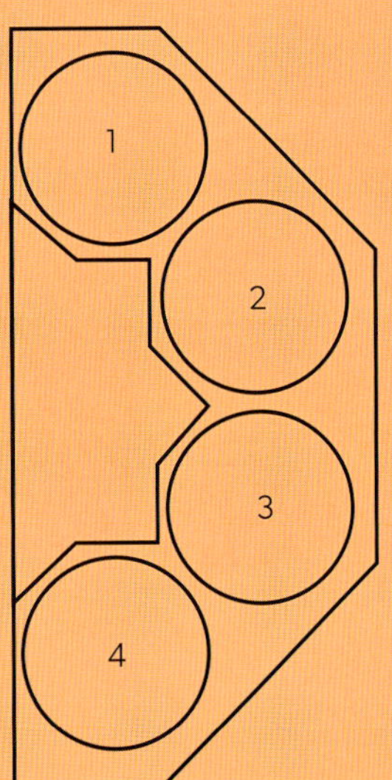

Motif 2

Row 7 (RS): Join Yarn B in first ch-sp, beg tr in same sp, ch1, [4tr in same sp, 1sc in next ch-sp, ch1, pc in ch3-sp from Rnd 5 and around slst from Rnd 6 together, ch1, 1sc in next ch-sp, 4tr in next ch-sp, ch3] 4 times, making ch1 instead of final ch3 on fourth rep, 1tr in same st, fasten off, do not turn. [4 pc, 34 tr, 8 sc, 11 ch3-sp, 2 ch1-sp]

Row 8 (RS): Join Yarn H in first ch-sp, 3sc in same sp, [3sc, 1hdc, 1dc, 1dc in next sc, 1hdc, 3sc, 3sc in next ch-sp] 4 times, fasten off and weave in ends. [8 dc, 8 hdc, 39 sc]

OUTER MEDALLIONS (MAKE 4)

Rnds 1–6: Work as for OM of Motif 1 .

Join Yarn H in next st and work Rnd 7 according to OM you are working.

Rnd 7 (OM 1): Work as for OM 1 of Motif 1, joining motif in position indicated on Placement Guide. Marking 37th st is unnecessary.

Rnd 7 (OM 2–4): Work as for OM 2 of Motif 1.

MOTIF BORDER

Row 1 (RS): Work as for Motif Border of Motif 1, starting in third sc of OM 4 and ending after fourth rep of pattern, omitting final dc on fourth rep, fasten off, do not turn. [84 dc, 16 hdc, 32 sc]

Row 2 (RS): With RS facing, join Yarn I in second st, beg tr in same st, [1tr, 1dc, 1hdc, 11sc, 3sc in next st, 11sc, 1hdc, 1dc, 1tr, ch1, sk4] 4 times, omitting final ch1 and sk4 on fourth rep, 1tr leaving final st unworked, fasten off and weave in ends. [10 tr, 8 dc, 8 hdc, 100 sc, 3 ch1-sp]

Motif 3 (make 5)

Rnds 1 and 2: With Yarn B, work as for Center Medallion of Motif 1, fasten off.

Rnd 3: Join Yarn C in final ch1-sp, work as for Center Medallion of Motif 1.

Rnd 4: Slst in first ch-sp, 1sc in same sp, [ch3, 1sc in next ch-sp] 15 times, ch3, slst in first sc, fasten off. [16 sc, 16 ch3-sp]

Rnd 5: Join Yarn D in first ch-sp, 1sc in same sp, [ch3, (3tr-cl, ch3, 3tr-cl) in next ch-sp, ch3, 1sc in next ch-sp] 8 times, omitting final sc on eighth rep, slst in first sc, fasten off. [16 3tr-cl, 8 sc, 24 ch3-sp]

Rnd 6: Join Yarn E in first ch-sp, 1sc in same sp, *[ch3, 1sc in next ch-sp] twice, ch3, sk 1 ch-sp, (4tr, ch3, 4tr) in next ch-sp, ch3, sk 1 ch-sp, 1sc in next ch-sp; rep from * 3 times more, omitting final sc on last rep, slst in first sc, fasten off. [32 tr, 12 sc, 20 ch3-sp]

Motif 3

Rnd 7: Join Yarn F in fourth ch-sp, beg dc in same sp, [ch3, 2dc in same sp, 4dc, 3dc in each of next 2 ch-sp, 1dc in next sc, 3dc in each of next 2 ch-sp, 4dc, 2dc in next ch-sp] 4 times, omitting final dc on fourth rep, slst in beg dc, fasten off. [100 dc, 4 ch2-sp]

Rnd 8: Join Yarn B in any ch-sp, beg dc in same sp, *4dc in same sp, [ch1, sk1, 1dc] 12 times, ch1, 1dc in next ch-sp; rep from * 3 times more, omitting final dc on last rep, fasten off. [68 dc, 52 ch-sp]

Rnd 9: Join Yarn I in third dc, 3sc in same st, [29sc, 3sc in next st] 4 times, omitting final 3sc on fourth rep, slst in first sc, fasten off and weave in ends. [128 sc]

Motif 4 (make 4)

Rows 3, 6, 7, 8, and 9 are all worked as RS rows. Join yarn where instructed with RS facing.

Row 1 (WS): With Yarn B, MR, beg dc, [ch1, 2dc-cl] 3 times, ch1, 1dc, turn. [3 2dc-cl, 2 dc, 4 ch1-sp]

Row 2: Beg dc, (ch1, 2dc-cl) twice in each of next 4 ch-sp, ch1, 1dc in final st, fasten off, do not turn. [8 2dc-cl, 2 dc, 9 ch-sp]

Row 3 (RS): Join Yarn C in first ch-sp, 1sc in same sp, [ch3, pc in next ch-sp, ch3, 1sc in next ch-sp] 4 times, turn. [4 pc, 5 sc, 8 ch3-sp]

Row 4: 1sc in first st, [ch3, 1sc in next ch-sp] 8 times, ch3, 1sc in final st, fasten off, turn. [10 sc, 9 ch-sp]

Row 5: Join Yarn D in first ch-sp, beg tr in same sp, ch1, [3tr-cl in same sp, ch3, 1sc in next ch-sp, ch3, 3tr-cl in next ch-sp, ch3] 4 times, making ch1 instead of final ch3 on fourth rep, 1tr in same ch-sp, fasten off, do not turn. [8 3tr-cl, 2 tr, 4 sc, 11 ch3-sp, 2 ch1-sp]

Row 6 (RS): Join Yarn E in first ch-sp, 1sc in same sp, *ch3, 1sc in next ch-sp, ch3, sk 1 ch-sp, (4tr, ch3, 4tr) in next ch-sp, ch3, sk 1 ch-sp, 1sc in next ch-sp, ch3, 1sc in next ch-sp; rep from * once more, fasten off, do not turn. [16 tr, 7 sc, 10 ch3-sp]

Row 7 (RS): Join Yarn F in first st, beg dc in same st, [3dc in each of next 2 ch-sp, 4dc, (2dc, ch3, 2dc) in next ch-sp, 4dc, 3dc in each of next 2 ch-sp, 1dc in next sc] twice, fasten off, do not turn. [51 dc, 2 ch3-sp]

Row 8 (RS): Join Yarn B in first st, beg dc in same st, *[1dc, ch1, sk1] 6 times, 5dc in next ch-sp, [ch1, sk1, 1dc] 6 times, ch1; rep from * once more, omitting final ch1, 1dc in final st, fasten off, do not turn. [36 dc, 25 ch1-sp]

Row 9 (RS): Join Yarn I in first st, 1sc in same st, 14sc, 3sc in next st, 29 sc, 3sc in next st, 15sc, fasten off and weave in ends. [65 sc]

Motif 5 (make 4)

Rows 3, 6, 7, 8, and 9 are all worked as RS rows. Join yarn where instructed with RS facing.

Row 1 (WS): With Yarn B, MR, beg dc, ch1, 2dc-cl, ch1, 1dc, turn. [1 2dc-cl, 2 dc, 2 ch1-sp]

Row 2: Beg dc, (ch1, 2dc-cl) twice in each of next 2 ch-sp, ch1, 1dc in final st, fasten off, do not turn. [4 2dc-cl, 2 dc, 5 ch1-sp]

Row 3 (RS): Join Yarn C in first ch-sp, 1sc in same sp, [ch3, pc in next ch-sp, ch3, 1sc in next ch-sp] twice, turn. [2 pc, 3 sc, 4 ch3-sp]

Row 4: 1sc in first st, [ch3, 1sc in next ch-sp] 4 times, ch3, 1sc in final st, fasten off, turn. [6 sc, 5 ch3-sp]

Row 5: Join Yarn D in first ch-sp, beg tr in same sp, ch1, [3tr-cl in same sp, ch3, 1sc in next sp, ch3, 3tr-cl in next sp, ch3] twice, making ch1 instead of final ch3 on second rep, 1tr in same sp, fasten off, do not turn. [4 3tr-cl, 2 tr, 2 sc, 5 ch3-sp, 2 ch1-sp]

Row 6 (RS): Join Yarn E in first ch-sp, 1sc in same sp, ch3, 1sc in next ch-sp, ch3, sk 1 ch-sp, (4tr, ch3, 4tr) in next ch-sp, ch3, sk 1 ch-sp, 1sc in next ch-sp, ch3, 1sc in next ch-sp, fasten off, do not turn. [8 tr, 4 sc, 5 ch3-sp]

Row 7 (RS): Join Yarn F in first st, beg dc in same st, 3dc in each of next 2 ch-sp, 4dc, (2dc, ch3, 2dc) in next ch-sp, 4dc, 3dc in each of next 2 ch-sp, 1dc in next sc, fasten off, do not turn. [26 dc, 1 ch3-sp]

Row 8 (RS): Join Yarn B in first st, beg dc in same st, [1dc, ch1, sk1] 6 times, 5dc in next ch-sp, [ch1, sk1, 1dc] 6 times, 1dc in final st, fasten off, do not turn. [19 dc, 12 ch1-sp]

Row 9 (RS): Join Yarn I in first st, 1sc in same st, 1 sc in each st/sp to center 5 dc, sk1, 3sc in next st, sk1, 1sc in each st/sp to end, fasten off and weave in ends. [33 sc]

Join the Motifs

With Yarn I, join motifs using Slip-stitch Join worked through both loops of both motifs with WS together (see General Techniques: Joining Methods). Treat ch1-sp at sides of Motifs A/B as a st when joining. Where a cnr meets 2 motifs, slst twice in both cnrs to secure them and avoid holes.

Make Blanket Border

On Rnd 1, work in side of any dc or tr sts.

Rnd 1: Join Yarn I in any cnr, *3sc in cnr, [2sc in next 2 dc, 1sc in next sc, 2sc in next ch-sp, 3sc in next tr, 1sc in next sc, 2sc in each of next 2 dc, 1sc in next sc, 3sc in next tr, 2sc in next dc, ch3, sk 4 sc on OM of Motif 2, 4sc, ch3, 1sc in final st of Center Medallion of Motif 2, 3sc in next 3 tr, 2sc in each of next 2 dc, 1dc in center ring, 2sc in each of next 2dc, 2sc in each of next 3 tr, 1sc in next sc, ch3, sk 4 sc on OM, ch3, 2sc in next dc, 3sc in next tr, 1sc in next sc on Motif 4, 2sc in each of next 2 dc, 1sc in next sc, 3sc in next tr, 2sc in next ch-sp, 1sc in next sc, 2sc in each of next 2 dc, 1sc in center ring] twice, omitting final sc on second rep; rep from * 3 times more, slst in first sc.

Rnd 2: [3sc in cnr st, 1sc in each st to next cnr, placing 4sc in each ch3-sp] 4 times, slst in first sc.

Rnd 3: Beg dc in cnr st, [ch2, 2dc in same st, 1dc in each st to cnr st, 2dc in cnr st] 4 times, omitting final dc on fourth rep, slst in beg dc.

Rnd 4: [3sc in cnr sp, 1sc in each sts to next cnr] 4 times, slst in first sc.

Rnd 5: Beg dc in cnr st, [ch1, 3dc in same st, (sk2, 3dc in next st) to next cnr, 3dc in cnr st] 4 times, omitting final dc on fourth rep, slst in beg dc.

Rnd 6: Beg 4dc-cl in cnr sp *[ch3, dc3tog over next 3 sts] to cnr sp, ch3, 4dc-cl in cnr sp; rep from * 3 times more, omitting final 4dc-cl on last rep, slst in beg 4dc-cl.

Rnd 7: [3sc in 3dc-cl, 3sc in ch-sp to cnr] 4 times, slst in first sc, fasten off and weave in ends.

Finishing

Weave in any rem ends and block blanket to given measurements and to open up lacy features.

Placement Guide

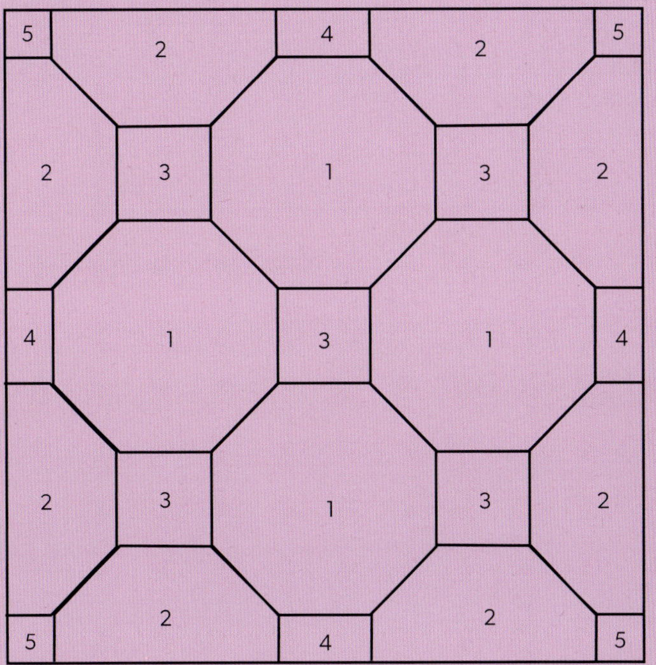

ANTIQUE PATINA BLANKET

Sometimes a quick make is just the thing you need, and at times it's best to enjoy a bit of slow crafting. This project is meant for mindful reflection. It is an homage to the traditional quilt block patterns of days long past. The main motifs are constructed to resemble log cabin quilt blocks, and the geometric striped motifs provide a contrasting bold sashing for an heirloom-quality piece.

Finished Size

58 x 50in (147.5 x 127cm)

Yarn

Worsted (aran) weight (#4 Medium)

Shown here: Malabrigo Rios (100% superwash Merino wool) 100g (210yd/192m; 1 hank each in following colors, unless otherwise specified:

- Yarn A: Archangel (850)
- Yarn B: Ankara Green (413)
- Yarn C: Kris (725)
- Yarn D: Ivy (138); 2 hanks
- Yarn E: Lettuce (037)
- Yarn F: Cucumber (708)
- Yarn G: Black (195); 4 hanks
- Yarn H: Sand Bank (131); 3 hanks

Hook

US size I/9 (5.5mm) hook

Gauge (Tension)

20 dc x 10 rows = 4 x 4in (10 x 10cm) using a US I/9 (5.5mm) hook.

Pattern Notes

Make all Motifs 1 and 2, then join using Motif 3 as instructed. Follow Placement Guide for colors used and order in which to join motifs.

To join new yarns, slst in specified stitch.

Make Blanket Body

Motif 1 (make 12)

Constructed by making a Base Square and adding on Log Cabin Sections 1–8 to complete.

BASE SQUARE

Rnd 1: With Yarn A, MR, beg dc, 11dc, slst in beg dc. [12 dc]

Rnd 2: Beg 4tr-cl, *ch4, 4tr-cl, [ch2, 4tr-cl] twice; rep from * 3 times more, omitting final 4tr-cl on last rep, slst in beg 4tr-cl. [12 4tr-cl, 4 ch4-sp, 8 ch2-sp]

Rnd 3: [5sc in ch-sp, 2sc in next ch-sp, 1sc in next st, 2sc in next ch-sp] 4 times, slst in first sc. [40 sc]

Rnd 4: Slst in cnr st, [3sc in cnr st, 9sc] 4 times, slst in first sc, fasten off. [48 sc]

Note: *Yarns used for Log Cabin Sections are shown in Placement Guide.*

LOG CABIN SECTION 1

Row 1 (RS): Join yarn in any cnr sc of Base Square, (beg dc, 1dc) in same st, [sk2, 3dc in next st] 3 times, sk2, 2dc in final st, turn. [13 dc]

Row 2: Beg dc, [3dc between groups of 3 dc] 4 times, 1dc in final st, turn. [14 dc]

Row 3: (Beg dc, 1dc) between first dc and next group of 3 dc, [3dc between groups of 3 dc] 3 times, 2dc between final group of 3 dc and final st, turn. [13 dc]

Row 4: Rep Row 2. [14 dc]

Fasten off.

Note: *With RS facing, rotate motif 90 degrees counterclockwise before beginning each section.*

LOG CABIN SECTIONS 2 AND 3 (MAKE 2)

Row 1 (RS): Join yarn in top right cnr of Base Square, (beg dc, 1dc) in same st, [sk2, 3dc in next st] 4 times, sk1, 3dc in side of next dc, sk1, 2dc in side of next dc, turn. [19 dc]

Row 2: Beg dc, [3dc between groups of 3 dc] to end, 1dc in final st, turn. [20 dc]

Motif 1

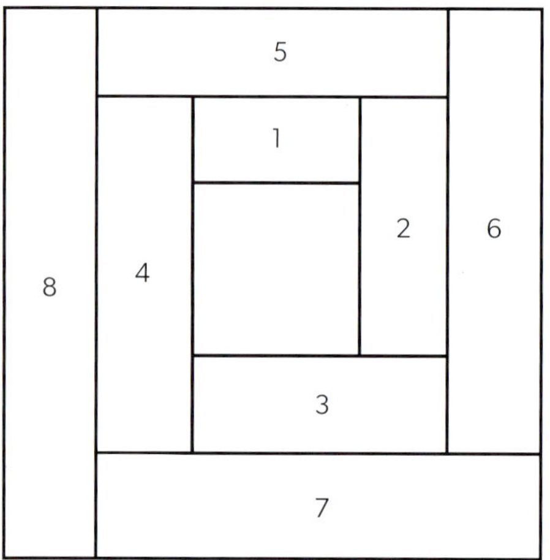

Motif 1 Chart

Motif 1 Base Square

Motif 1

Row 3: (Beg dc, 1dc) between first dc and first group of 3 dc, [3dc between groups of 3 dc] to final st, 2dc between final group of 3 dc and final st, turn. [19 dc]

Row 4: Rep Row 2, fasten off. [20 dc]

LOG CABIN SECTION 4

Row 1: Join yarn in top right dc, (beg dc, 1dc) in side of same st, 3dc in side of next st, 3dc in top left cnr sc of Base Square, [sk2, 3dc in next st] 4 times, 3dc in side of next st, 2dc in side of next st, turn. [25 dc]

Row 2 and 3: Work as for Rows 2 and 3 of Section 2. [25 dc]

Row 4: Rep Row 2, fasten off. [26 dc]

LOG CABIN SECTION 5

Row 1: Join yarn in side of top right dc, (beg dc, 1dc) in same sp, 3dc in each of next 2 sp, [3dc between groups of 3 dc] 3 times, 3dc in each of next 2 sp, 2dc in next sp, turn. [25 dc]

Row 2: Work as for Row 2 of Section 2. [26 dc]

Row 3: Work as for Row 3 of Section 2. [25 dc]

Row 4: Rep Row 2. [26 dc]

Fasten off.

LOG CABIN SECTIONS 6 AND 7 (MAKE 2)

Row 1: Join yarn in top right ch-sp, (beg dc, 1dc) in same sp, 3dc in each of next 2 sp, [3dc between groups of 3 dc] 5 times, 3dc in each of next 2 sp, 2dc in next sp, turn. [31 dc]

Row 2: Work as for Row 2 of Section 2. [32 dc]

Row 3: Work as for Row 3 of Section 2. [31 dc]

Row 4: Rep Row 2. [32 dc]

Fasten off.

LOG CABIN SECTION 8

Row 1: Join yarn in top right ch-sp, (beg dc, 1dc) in same sp, 3dc in each of next 2 sp, [3dc between groups of 3 dc] 7 times, 3dc in each of next 2 sp, 2dc in next sp, turn. [37 dc]

Row 2: Work as for Row 2 of Section 2. [38 dc]

Row 3: Work as for Row 3 of Section 2. [37 dc]

Row 4: Rep Row 2. [38 dc]

Fasten off.

Border Rnd: Join Yarn G in top right cnr, [3sc in cnr st, 38sc evenly to next cnr st] 4 times, slst in first sc, fasten off and weave in ends.

Make another 11 Motif 1 blocks using colors shown on Placement Guide.

Motif 2 (make 12)

Rnd 1: With Yarn G, MR, beg tr, [3dc, 1tr] 3 times, 3dc, slst in beg tr. [4 tr, 12 dc]

Rnd 2: Beg tr in same st as slst, [2dc in same st, 3dc, (2dc, 1tr) in next st] 4 times, omitting final tr on last rep, slst in beg tr, fasten off. [16 dc inc]

Rnd 3: Rep Rnd 2. [4 tr, 44 dc]

Rnd 4: [3sc in cnr tr, 11sc] 4 times, slst in first sc, fasten off. [56 sc]

Rnd 5: [3sc in cnr tr, 15sc] 4 times, slst in first sc, fasten off. [68 sc]

Motif 3 (make 25)

Motif 3 joins all motifs around it; when all 3 motifs are complete, Blanket Body is fully joined. Alternate Yarns H and G every 2 rows. Carry non-working yarn up sides of motif.

Row 1 (RS): With Yarn H, ch14, 1dc in third ch from hook (turning ch counts as 1 dc), 11dc, turn. [13 dc]

Row 2–4: Beg dc, 12dc, fasten off, turn.

Row 5: Join Yarn G in first st, beg dc, 12dc, turn.

Rows 6–20: Beg dc, 12dc, turn, alternating yarns every 4 rows, ending with Yarn H.

Fasten off Yarn G. Cont to Border Rnd with Yarn H.

Border Rnd: With Yarn H, 2sc in cnr st, make PLT Join (see General Techniques: Joining Methods) through cnr sts of Motifs 2 and 1, 1sc in same cnr st, [PLT in next st on Motif 2, 1sc on Motif 3] 11 times, PLT, 1sc in cnr st, PLT, 1sc in same cnr st, PLT through cnr sts of Motifs 2 and 1, 1sc in same cnr st, [PLT on Motif 1, 1sc on Motif 3] 38 times, working 2sc per dc st across side and making 38 PLT evenly across Motif 1, 1sc in cnr st, PLT on Motif 1, 1sc in same cnr st, PLT in cnr sts of Motifs 1 and 2, 1sc in same cnr st, work across rem 2 sides, joining to Motifs 2 and 1 as before until first sc is reached, slst in first sc, fasten off, bring yarn tail to back of work through next st on Motif 1 to join it, weave in ends.

Motif 3

Placement Guide

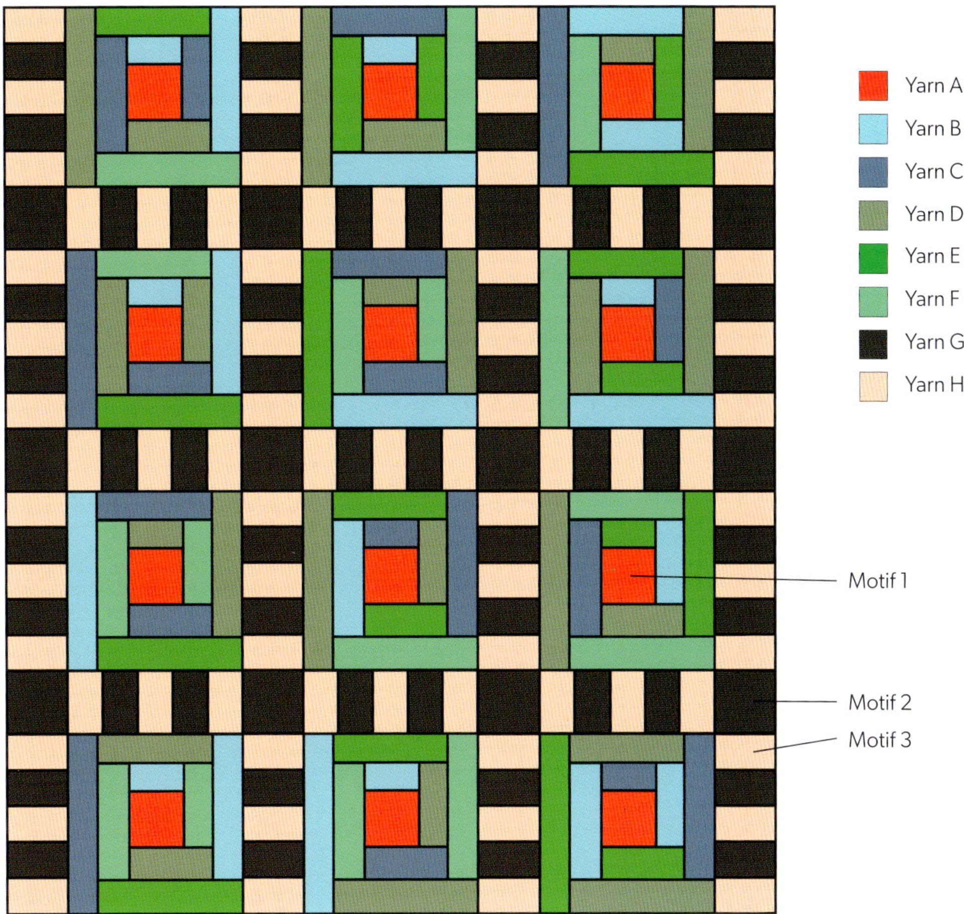

Make Blanket Border

Rnd 1: Join Yarn G in top right cnr of blanket, [3sc in cnr, 1sc in each st across to next cnr] 4 times, being sure to make same number of sc on opposite sides, slst in first sc.

Rnd 2: [3sc in cnr st, 1sc in each st across to next cnr] 4 times, slst in first sc, fasten off.

Finishing

Weave in any rem ends and block blanket to given measurements and to flatten seams.

CHRYSALIS BLANKET

If you're ready for a simple blanket that packs a big visual punch, this is the make for you! The Chrysalis Blanket is a tribute to transformation and the unbreakable human spirit. Butterflies are a perfect representation of the cycle of life, and I have brought these images to a blanket design that will invigorate your crafting time.

Finished Size

72 x 72in (183 x 183cm)

Yarn

Worsted (aran) weight (#4 Medium)

Shown here: Scheepjes Chunky Monkey (100% premium acrylic) 100g (127yd/116m); 3 balls each in following colors, unless otherwise specified:

- Yarn A: Scarlet (1010)
- Yarn B: Coral (1132)
- Yarn C: Orange (2002)
- Yarn D: Peach (1026)
- Yarn E: Stone (2017); 8 balls
- Yarn F: Mint (1020)
- Yarn G: Fern (2016)
- Yarn H: Aqua (1422)
- Yarn I: Air Force Blue (1302)
- Yarn J: Purple (1425)
- Yarn K: Evergreen (1062); 8 balls

Hook

US size I/9 (5.5mm) hook

Gauge (Tension)

13 dc x 6 rows = 4 x 4in (10 x 10cm) using a US I/9 (5.5mm) hook.

Pattern Notes

Motif 1 blocks are joined in rows as you go, using PLT Join (see General Techniques: Joining Methods) on Motif Border Rnd. Motif 2 and Motif 3 blocks are worked and joined onto blanket on final rnd/row.

To join new yarns, slst in specified stitch.

Make Blanket Body

The top left Motif 1 is the first motif, worked completely without joining. Subsequent Motif 1s are joined as you go on the Border Rnd, from left to right and top to bottom. Finally Motifs 2 and 3 are joined.

Placement Guide

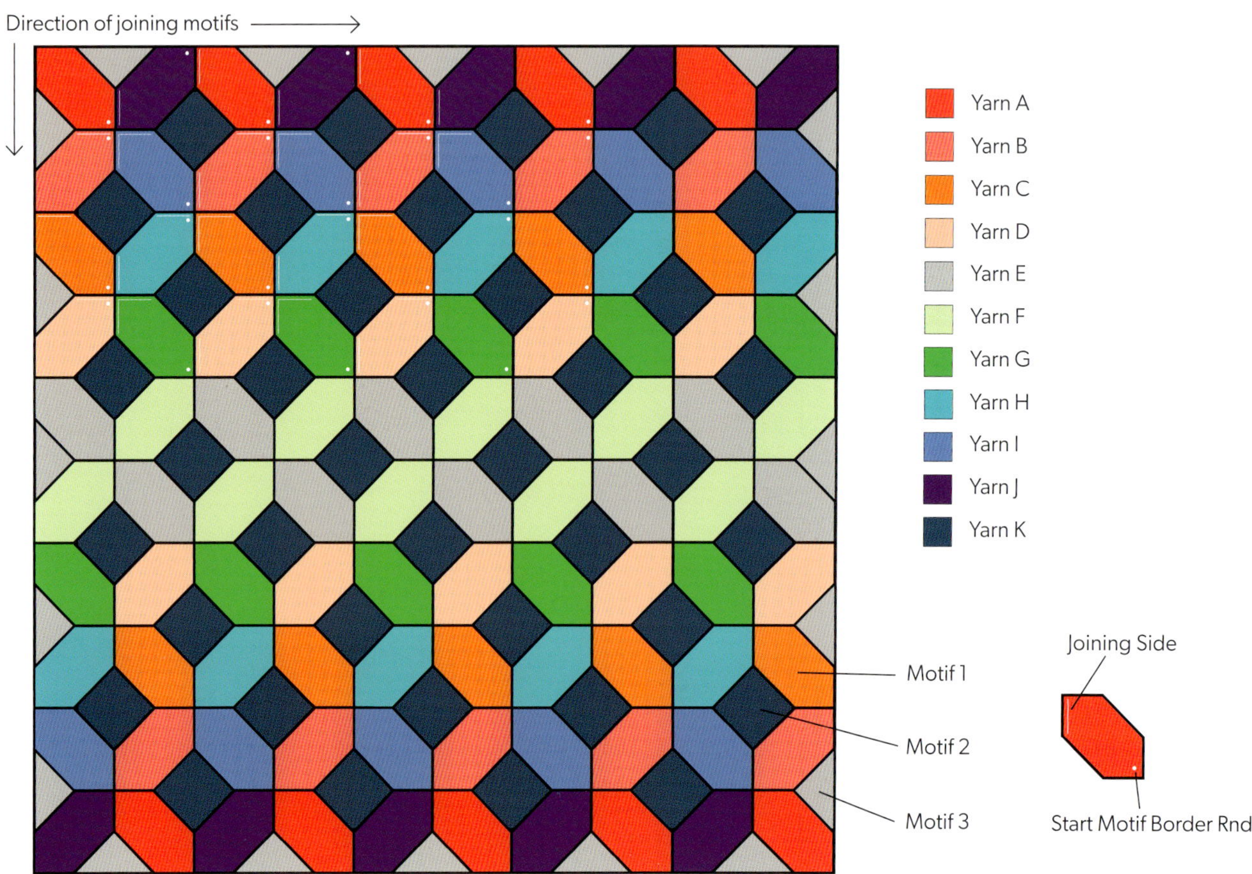

Motif 1

Make 10 of each color except Yarn K.

Row 1 (RS): MR, [1sc, ch1] twice, 1sc, turn. [3 sc, 2 ch1-sp]

Row 2: (1sc, ch1, 1sc) in first ch-sp, ch1, (1sc, ch1, 1sc) in final ch-sp, turn. [4 sc, 3 ch1-sp]

Row 3: (1sc, ch1, 1sc) in first ch-sp, ch1, 1sc in next ch-sp, ch1, (1sc, ch1, 1sc) in final ch-sp, turn. [5 sc, 4 ch1-sp]

Row 4: (1sc, ch1, 1sc) in first ch-sp, [ch1, 1sc in next ch-sp] to final ch-sp, ch1, (1sc, ch1, 1sc) in final ch-sp, turn. [1 sc and 1 ch1-sp inc]

Rows 5–9: Rep Row 4 another 5 times, turn. [11 sc, 10 ch1-sp]

Rows 10–26: [Ch1, 1sc in next ch-sp] to end, turn. PM at beg and end of Rows 10 and 26. [10 sc, 10 ch1-sp]

Rows 27–35: [1sc in next ch-sp, ch1] to final ch-sp, 1sc in final ch-sp, turn. [2 sc, 1 ch1-sp]

Row 36: 1sc in ch-sp, do not turn, cont to Motif Border Rnd.

Note: *First motif is at top left of blanket and completed without joining. Join rem motifs as instructed, working in rows across and down blanket.*

Motif Border Rnd (first motif): 3sc in sc from Row 36, 9sc evenly to marked st, 3sc in marked st, 13sc evenly to next marked st, 3sc in marked st, 9sc evenly to starting ring, 3sc in ring, 9sc to next marked st, 3sc in marked st, 13sc to next marked st, 3sc in marked st, 9sc to beg, slst in first sc, fasten off and weave in ends. [80 sc]

Motif Border Rnd (all rem motifs): Work as for first motif, but on joining sides (see Placement Guide), replace *3sc, 9sc, 3sc* with *2sc in marked st, PLT (see General Techniques: Joining Methods) in cnr sc on completed motif, 1sc in same marked st, [PLT, 1sc] 9 times, PLT, 1sc in next marked st, PLT, 2sc in same marked st*, then finish rnd, slst in first sc, fasten off and weave in ends.

Note: *When 2 consecutive sides are joined, join first side up to cnr sc, PLT in cnr sc of diagonal completed motif to close hole, cont to join second side, then finish the rnd, slst in first sc, fasten off and weave in ends.*

Cont working and joining Motif 1 blocks in rows across and down the blanket until all are completed and joined.

Motif 1 Chart

Motif 1

Motif 2

Make 40 with Yarn K.

Rnd 1: MR, beg dc, [ch1, 3dc] 3 times, ch1, 2dc, slst in beg dc. [12 dc, 4 ch1-sp]

Rnd 2: Beg dc in ch-sp, [ch1, 3dc in same sp, 3dc in next ch-sp] 4 times, omitting final dc on fourth rep, slst in beg dc. [24 dc, 4 ch1-sp]

Rnd 3: Beg dc in ch-sp, [ch1, 3dc in same sp, 3dc between groups of 3 dc, 3dc in next ch-sp] 4 times, omitting final dc on fourth rep, slst in beg dc. [36 dc, 4 ch1-sp]

Rnd 4: Beg dc in ch-sp, [ch1, 3dc in same sp, 3dc between groups of 3 dc, ch1, 3dc between groups of 3 dc, 3dc in next ch-sp] 4 times, omitting final dc on fourth rep, slst in beg dc. [48 dc, 8 ch1-sp]

***Note:** Rnd 5 is joining rnd. All sts are joined with PLT Join to surrounding completed motifs. After every st, PLT in corresponding st on adjacent motif.*

Rnd 5: [3sc in ch-sp, 13sc] 4 times, slst in first sc, fasten off and weave in ends. [64 sc]

Motif 2 Chart

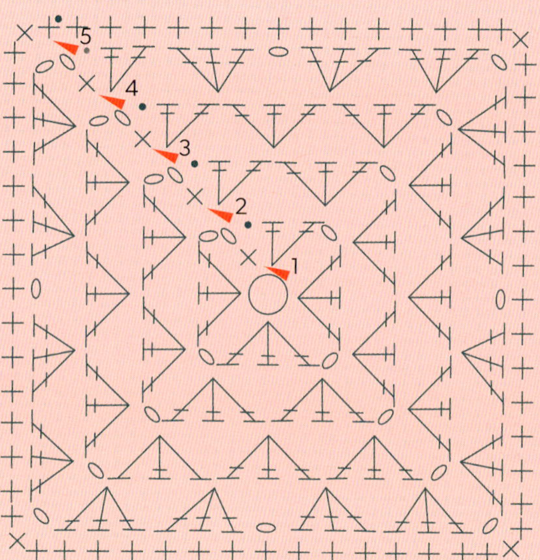

Motif 2

Motif 3

Make 20 with Yarn E.

Row 1 (RS): MR, beg dc, [ch1, 3dc] twice, ch1, 1dc, turn. [8 dc, 3 ch1-sp]

Row 2: Beg dc in ch-sp, [ch1, 3dc in same sp, 3dc in next ch-sp] twice, ch1, 1dc in same sp, turn. [14 dc, 3 ch1-sp]

Row 3: Beg dc in ch-sp, [ch1, 3dc in same sp, 3dc between groups of 3 dc, 3dc in next ch-sp] twice, ch1, 1dc in same sp. [20 dc, 3 ch1-sp]

Row 4: Beg dc in ch-sp, [ch1, 3dc in same sp, 3dc between groups of 3 dc, ch1, 3dc between groups of 3 dc, 3dc in next ch-sp] twice, ch1, 1dc in same sp. [26 dc, 5 ch1-sp]

Note: *On Row 5, after every st work PLT in corresponding st on adjacent motif.*

Row 5: 2sc in ch-sp, 13sc, 3sc in ch-sp, 13sc, 2sc, fasten off and weave in ends. [33 sc]

Motif 3 Chart

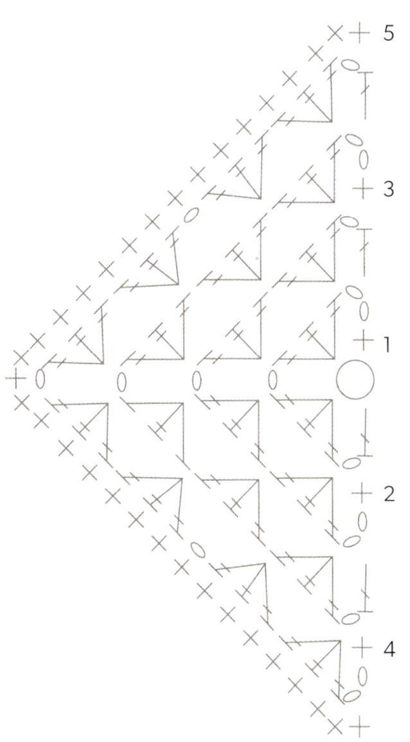

Make Blanket Border

Join Yarn E to any cnr.

Blanket Border Rnd: *3sc in cnr, [12sc across Motif 1, 18sc across Motif 3, 12sc across Motif 1] 5 times; rep from * 3 times more, slst in first sc.

Rnd 2: Beg dc in cnr sc, [4dc in same st, 1dc in each st to next cnr, 1dc in cnr st] 4 times, omitting final dc on fourth rep, slst in beg dc, fasten off and weave in ends.

Finishing

Weave in any rem ends and block blanket to given measurements and to flatten seams.

FIELD OF BLOOMS BLANKET

This design is a celebration of color and simple, precious motifs, with the added surprise of sections worked back and forth incorporated into the layout. You will adore playing with color and working up these quick motifs on the go or in your favorite crafting chair, and then adding in the clever back-and-forth sections. What a treat!

Finished Size

47 x 42in (119.5 x 106.5cm)

Yarn

Worsted (aran) weight (#4 Medium)

Shown here: Knit Picks Swish Worsted (100% fine superwash Merino wool) 50g (110yd/100m); 1 ball each in following colors:

Color group 1

- Yarn 1A: Frosting
- Yarn 1B: Blossom Heather
- Yarn 1C: Rose Heather
- Yarn 1D: Hollyberry

Color group 2

- Yarn 2A: Honey
- Yarn 2B: Clementine
- Yarn 2C: Allspice
- Yarn 2D: Copper

Color group 3

- Yarn 3A: Wonderland Heather
- Yarn 3B: Estuary Heather
- Yarn 3C: Voyage Heather
- Yarn 3D: Rainforest Heather

Color group 4

- Yarn 4A: Arctic
- Yarn 4B: Electric Blue
- Yarn 4C: Gulfstream
- Yarn 4D: Marine Heather

Hook

- US size G/7 (4.5mm) hook
- US size G/7 (4mm hook) for border

Gauge (Tension)

18 dc x 9 rows = 4 x 4in (10 x 10cm) using a US G/7 (4.5mm) hook.

Pattern Notes

Motifs are completed before joining. Leave a long tail on each for Whip-stitch Join (see General Techniques: Joining Methods).

Weave in ends as you go for quick finish.

To join new yarns, slst in specified stitch.

Make Blanket Body

For each of the four color groups, work 12 assorted motifs, 48 in total. For each motif number work across the table for the color sequence to use.

Motif 1 (make 16)

Make 4 in each color group.

Rnd 1: With C1, MR, beg dc, 15dc, slst in beg dc, fasten off. [16 dc]

Rnd 2: Join C2 in any st, beg 2dc-cl, [ch2, 2dc-cl] 15 times, ch2, slst in beg 2dc-cl, fasten off. [16 2dc-cl, 16 ch2-sp]

Rnd 3: Join C3 in any ch-sp, beg 4tr-cl in same sp, [ch3, 4tr-cl in next ch-sp] 15 times, ch3, slst in beg 4tr-cl, fasten off. [16 4tr-cl, 16 ch3-sp]

Rnd 4: Join C4 in any ch-sp, beg tr in same sp, [ch3, 3tr in same sp, 3dc in next ch-sp, 3sc in next ch-sp, 3dc in next ch-sp, 3tr in next ch-sp] 4 times, omitting final tr on fourth rep, slst in beg tr. [24 tr, 24 dc, 12 sc, 4 ch3-sp]

Rnd 5: [5sc in ch-sp, 15sc] 4 times, slst in first sc, fasten off leaving long tail, and weave in rem ends. [80 sc]

Motif 2 (make 8)

Make 4 in each of color groups 2 and 3.

Rnd 1: With C1, MR, beg 2dc-cl, [ch2, 2dc-cl] 7 times, ch2, slst in beg 2dc-cl, fasten off. [8 2dc-cl, 8 ch2-sp]

Rnd 2: Join C2 in any ch-sp, beg 4tr-cl in same sp, [ch3, 4tr-cl in next ch-sp] 7 times, ch3, slst in beg 4tr-cl, fasten off. [8 4tr-cl, 8 ch3-sp]

Rnd 3: Join C3 any ch-sp, beg 4dc-cl in same sp, [ch3, 4dc-cl in same ch-sp, ch3, 4dc-cl in next ch-sp] 8 times, omitting final 4dc-cl on eighth rep, ch3, slst in beg 4tr-cl, fasten off. [16 4dc-cl, 16 ch3-sp]

Rnd 4: Join C4 in first ch-sp, beg tr in same sp, [ch3, 3tr in same sp, 3dc in next ch-sp, 3sc in next ch-sp, 3dc in next ch-sp, 3tr in next ch-sp] 4 times, omitting final tr on fourth rep, slst in beg tr. [24 tr, 24 dc, 12 sc, 4 ch3-sp]

Rnd 5: [5sc in ch-sp, 15sc] 4 times, slst in first sc, fasten off leaving long tail, and weave in rem ends. [80 sc]

Motif Color Table

Motifs	C1	C2	C3	C4
1, 3, 5	1A	1B	1C	1A
1, 2, 4	2B	2C	2D	2B
1, 2, 6	3C	3B	3A	3C
1, 3, 4	4D	4C	4B	4D

Motif 1

Motif 2

Motif 3

Motif 4

Motif 3 (make 8)

Make 4 in each of color groups 1 and 4.

Rnd 1: With C1, MR, beg dc, 15dc, slst in beg dc, fasten off, turn. [16 dc]

Note: *Tr sts on Rnd 2 form tiny bobbles on RS of work.*

Rnd 2 (WS): Join C2 in any st, [1sc, 1tr] in each st to end, slst in first sc, fasten off, turn. [16 tr, 16 sc]

Rnd 3 (RS): Join C3 in any sc, beg 2tr-cl in same st, [ch3, 2tr-cl in next sc] 15 times, ch3, slst in beg 2tr-cl. [16 2tr-cl, 16 ch3-sp]

Rnd 4: 5sc in each ch-sp to end, slst in first sc, fasten off. [80 sc]

Rnd 5: Join C4 in third sc, beg tr in same st, [ch3, 3tr in same st, sk4, 3dc in next st, sk4, 3sc in next st, sk4, 3dc in next st, sk4, 3tr in next st] 4 times, omitting final tr on fourth rep, slst in beg tr. [24 tr, 24 dc, 12 sc, 4 ch3-sp]

Rnd 6: [5sc in ch-sp, 15sc] 4 times, slst in first sc, fasten off leaving long tail, and weave in rem ends. [80 sc]

Note: *For Motifs 4–6, all Rows are worked on RS, without turning, unless otherwise stated. Attach new yarn with RS facing on each row.*

Motif 4 (make 8)

Make 4 in each of color groups 2 and 4.

Row 1 (RS): With C1, MR, beg dc, 8dc, fasten off. [16 dc]

Row 2: Join C2 in first st, beg 2dc-cl in first st, [ch2, 2dc-cl] 8 times, fasten off. [9 2dc-cl, 8 ch2-sp]

Row 3: Join C3 in first st, beg tr in same st, ch2, [4tr-cl in next ch-sp, ch3] 7 times, 4tr-cl in final ch-sp, ch2, 1tr in final st, fasten off. [8 4tr-cl, 2 tr, 2 ch2-sp, 7 ch3-sp]

Row 4: Join C4 in first ch-sp, beg tr in same sp, ch2, [3tr in same sp, 3dc in next ch-sp, 3sc in next ch-sp, 3dc in next ch-sp, 3tr in next ch-sp, ch3] twice, omitting final ch3 on second rep, ch2, 1tr in same sp, fasten off. [14 tr, 12 dc, 6 sc, 2 ch2-sp, 1 ch3-sp]

Row 5: Rejoin C4 in first ch-sp, 3sc in same sp, 15sc, 5sc in next ch-sp, 15sc, 3sc in final ch-sp, fasten off leaving long tail, and weave in rem ends. [41 sc]

Motif 5 (make 4)

Make 4 with color group 1.

Row 1: With C1, MR, beg 2dc-cl, [ch2, 2dc-cl] 4 times, fasten off. [5 2dc-cl, 4 ch2-sp]

Row 2: Join C2 in first st, beg tr in same st, ch2, [4tr-cl in next ch-sp, ch3] 3 times, 4tr-cl, ch2, 1tr in final st, fasten off. [4 4tr-cl, 2 tr, 2 ch2-sp, 3 ch3-sp]

Row 3: Join C3 in first st, beg dc in same st, ch2, 4dc-cl in ch-sp, [ch3, 4dc-cl in next ch-sp, ch3, 4dc-cl in same ch-sp] 3 times, ch3, 4dc-cl in ch-sp, ch2, 1dc in final st, fasten off. [8 4dc-cl, 2 dc, 2 ch2-sp, 7 ch3-sp]

Row 4: Join C4 in first ch-sp, beg tr in same sp, ch2, [3tr in same sp, 3dc in next ch-sp, 3sc in next ch-sp, 3dc in next ch-sp, 3tr in next ch-sp, ch3] twice, omitting final ch3 on second rep, ch2, 1tr in same ch-sp, fasten off. [14 tr, 12 dc, 6 sc, 2 ch2-sp, 1 ch3-sp]

Row 5: Rejoin C4 in first ch-sp, 3sc in same sp, 15sc, 5sc in next ch-sp, 15sc, 3sc in final ch-sp, fasten off leaving long tail, and weave in rem ends. [41 sc]

Motif 5

Motif 6 (make 4)

Make 4 with color group 3.

Row 1: With C1, MR, beg dc, 7dc, fasten off, turn. [8 dc]

***Note:** Tr sts on Row 2 form tiny bobbles on RS of work.*

Row 2 (WS): With WS facing, join C2 in first st, (1sc, 1tr) in each of next 7 sts, 1sc in final st, fasten off, turn. [7 tr, 8 sc]

Row 3 (RS): With RS facing, join C3 in first sc, (beg tr, ch2, 2tr-cl) in same st, [ch3, 2tr-cl in next sc] 7 times, ch2, 1tr in final sc, fasten off. [8 2tr-cl, 2 tr, 2 ch2-sp, 7 ch3-sp]

Row 4: Rejoin C3 in first ch-sp, 3sc in same sp, 5sc in each of next 7 ch-sp, 3sc in final ch-sp, fasten off. [41 sc]

Row 5: Join C4 in first sc, beg tr in same st, ch2, [3tr in same st, sk4, 3dc in next st, sk4, 3sc in next st, sk4, 3dc in next st, sk4, 3tr in next st, ch3] twice, omitting final ch3 on second rep, ch2, 1tr in same st. [14 tr, 12 dc, 6 sc, 2 ch2-sp, 1 ch3-sp]

Row 6: Rejoin C4 in first ch-sp, 3sc in same sp, 15sc, 5sc in next ch-sp, 15sc, 3sc in final ch-sp, fasten off leaving long tail, and weave in rem ends. [41 sc]

Motif 6

Fill Triangle 1

Row 1 (RS): With Yarn 1D, slst in final st of final Row of Motif 4, 23sc evenly across each of 4 motifs, 1sc in same st, turn. [93 sc]

Row 2 (WS): 1sc in first st, [ch5, sk3, 1sc] 23 times, fasten off, turn. [24 sc, 23 ch5-sp]

Row 3: Join Yarn 1A in first ch-sp, 1sc in same sp, *([2tr-cl, ch2] 3 times, 2tr-cl) in next ch-sp, 1sc in next ch-sp; rep from * to end, turn. [44 2tr-cl, 12 sc, 33 ch2-sp]

Row 4: Slst in first ch-sp, 1sc in same sp, [ch5, sk 1 ch-sp, 1sc in next ch-sp, ch5, 1sc in next ch-sp] to last 2 ch-sp, ch5, sk 1 ch-sp, 1sc in final ch-sp, fasten off, turn.

Row 5: With Yarn 2D, slst around second ch2-sp from 2 rows below and first ch5-sp 1 row below at the same time, 1sc around both ch-sp together, *([2trcl, ch2] 3 times, 2trcl) in next ch-sp, 1sc in next ch-sp; rep from * to end, turn.

Row 6: Rep Row 4.

On Rows 7–23, change color at the start of every RS row in this order: 4A, 4D, 1B, 2C, 4B, 4D, 2D, 2C, 3C.

Rows 7–22: Rep Rows 5 and 6 another 8 times.

Row 23: Rep Row 5, fasten off and weave in ends.

Fill Triangle 2

Join Yarn 1D in final st of final Row of Motif 4, and work as for Fill Triangle A using yarns in this order: 3A, 2A, 4D, 4A, 2B, 2C, 4B, 4A, 1B, 1A, 1D.

Fill Triangle 3

Fill Triangle 3

Row 1 (RS): Join Yarn 1D in final st of final row of Motif 4, 23sc evenly across each of 8 motifs, 1sc in same st, turn. [185 sc]

Row 2: 1sc in first st, [ch5, sk3, 1sc] 46 times, fasten off, turn. [47 sc, 46 ch5-sp]

Row 3: Join Yarn 2A in first ch-sp, 1sc in same sp, *([2tr-cl, ch2] 3 times, 2tr-cl) in next ch-sp, 1sc in next ch-sp; rep from * to center sc, 1sc in next ch-sp, rep from * to end, turn. [44 2tr-cl, 12 sc, 33 ch2-sp]

Row 4: Slst in first ch-sp, 1sc in same sp, [ch5, sk 1 ch-sp, 1sc in next ch-sp, ch5, 1sc in next ch-sp] until 2 ch-sp rem before center 2 sc, ch5, sk 1 ch-sp, 1sc in each of next 2 ch-sp, [ch5, sk 1 ch-sp, 1sc in next ch-sp, ch5, 1sc in next ch-sp] until 2 ch-sp rem, ch5, sk 1 ch-sp, 1sc in final ch-sp, fasten off, turn.

Row 5: With Yarn 3A slst around second ch2-sp from 2 rows below and first ch5-sp of previous row at the same time, 1sc around both ch-sp together, *([2tr-cl, ch2] 3 times, 2tr-cl) in next ch-sp, 1sc in next ch-sp; rep from * to center ch-sp, 1sc in next ch-sp, rep from * to end, turn.

Row 6: Rep Row 4.

On Rows 7–23, change color at the start of every RS row in this order: 1A, 2D, 3C, 1A, 1D, 2B, 1B, 3C, 1D.

Rows 7–22: Rep Rows 5 and 6 another 8 times.

Row 23: Rep Row 5, fasten off and weave in ends.

Join the Motifs

The Placement Guide shows the color group, Motifs 1–6, and the color of the Rnd/Row. Lay out the motifs accordingly. With a long tail or short piece of the same color yarn if needed, Whip-stitch Join adjacent motifs together through both loops with motifs held WS together (see General Techniques: Joining Methods). Weave in all ends.

Make Blanket Border

Rnd 1: Join Yarn 3B in top right cnr, 3sc in cnr, 167sc evenly across short side, 5sc in cnr, 188sc evenly across long side, change to Yarn 4D, 3sc in cnr, 168sc evenly across short side, 3sc in cnr, 188sc evenly across long side, 2 sc in first cnr, slst in first sc, fasten off.

Rnd 2: With Yarn 3B and smaller hook, slst in top right cnr, [3sc in cnr, 1sc in each st to next cnr] 4 times, slst in first sc, fasten off and weave in ends.

Finishing

Weave in any rem ends and block blanket to given measurements and to open up lacy features.

Placement Guide

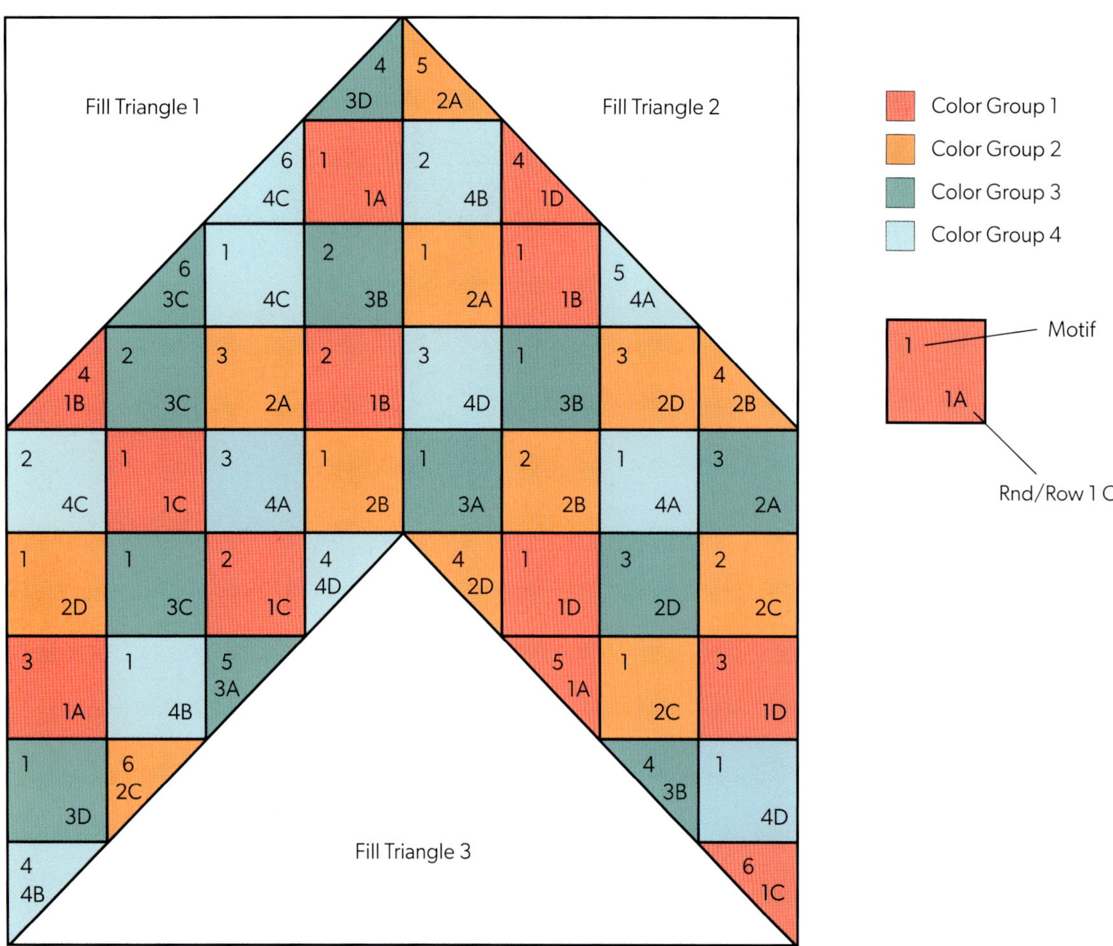

DESERT DREAMS BLANKET

Nothing beats a fresh, giftable blanket pattern, and this blanket makes the perfect present. The color palette can be adjusted to suit any aesthetic, and with the eye-catching design, they'll never know you worked it up so quickly. The mix of floral motifs and elongated diamonds paired with a modern twist on the granny square will keep you entertained from start to finish.

Finished Size

43 x 35in (109 x 89cm)

Yarn

Worsted (aran) weight (#4 Medium)

Shown here: Knit Picks Brava Tweed (97% premium acrylic, 3% viscose) 100g (218yd/200m); 1 ball each in following colors, unless otherwise specified:

- Yarn A: Rosefinch; 2 balls
- Yarn B: Wasabi
- Yarn C: Boysenberry
- Yarn D: Stratus
- Yarn E: Mink

Hook

- US size I/9 (5.5mm) hook
- US size G/6 (4mm) for border

Gauge (Tension)

13 dc x 6.5 rows = 4 x 4in (10 x 10cm) using a US I/9 (5.5mm) hook.

Pattern Notes

Motifs are completed before joining. Leave a long tail on each to use for Whip-stitch Join (see General Techniques: Joining Methods).

To join new yarns, slst in specified stitch.

Make Blanket Body

Motifs 1 and 2

Make 5 of Motif 1: C1: Yarn A, C2: Yarn C, C3: Yarn D.

Make 8 of Motif 2: C1: Yarn C, C2, Yarn A, C3: Yarn E.

Rnd 1: With C1, MR, beg 2dc-cl, [ch2, 2dc-cl] 7 times, ch2, slst in beg 2dc-cl, fasten off. [8 2dc-cl, 8 ch2-sp]

Rnd 2: Join Yarn C2 in any ch-sp, beg dc in same sp, [4dc in same sp, ch1, 1dc in next ch-sp] 8 times, omitting final dc on eighth rep, slst in beg dc. [40 dc, 8 ch1-sp]

Rnd 3: Beg dc5tog over first 5 sts, [ch5, dc5tog] 7 times, ch5, slst in beg dc5tog, fasten off. [8 dc5tog, 8 ch5-sp]

Rnd 4: Join C3 in any dc5tog, [FPsc in dc5tog, ch2, 1dc in ch5-sp and ch-sp from Rnd 2 together, ch2] 8 times, slst in first FPsc. [8 FPsc, 8 dc, 16 ch2-sp]

Rnd 5: Slst in ch-sp, 3sc in same sp, [3sc in each of next 3 ch-sp, ch3, 3sc in next ch-sp] 4 times, omitting final 3sc on fourth rep, slst in first sc. [48 sc, 4 ch3-sp]

Rnd 6: [12sc, 5sc in cnr sp] 4 times, slst in first sc, fasten off and weave in ends. [68 sc]

Motifs 3 and 4

Make 5 of Motif 3: C1: Yarn A; C2: Yarn C; C3: Yarn D.

Make 4 of Motif 4: C1: Yarn C; C2: Yarn A; C3: Yarn E.

Row 1 (RS): With Yarn A, MR, beg dc, [ch2, 2dc-cl] 4 times, ch2, 1dc, fasten off, turn. [4 2dc-cl, 2dc, 5 ch2-sp]

Row 2: Join Yarn C in first ch-sp, beg dc in same sp, [2dc in same sp, ch1, 3dc in next ch-sp] 4 times, turn. [21 dc, 4 ch1-sp]

Row 3: Beg dc3tog, [ch5, dc5tog] 3 times, ch5, dc3tog, fasten off, do not turn. [3 dc5tog, 2 dc4tog, 4 ch-sp]

Join Yarn D in first dc3tog, ready to work another RS row.

Row 4 (RS): FPsc in first dc3tog, [ch2, 1dc in ch5-sp and ch1-sp from Row 2 together, ch2, FPsc in dc5tog] 4 times, working final FPsc in final dc3tog, turn. [5 FPsc, 4 dc, 8 ch2-sp]

Motif 1

Row 5: Beg dc in first st, ch1, 3sc in next 4 ch-sp, ch3, 3sc in next 4 ch-sp, ch1, 1dc in final st, turn. [2 dc, 24 sc, 2 ch1-sp, 1 ch3-sp]

Row 6: 3sc in cnr sp, 12sc, 5sc in cnr sp, 12sc, 3sc in cnr sp, fasten off and weave in ends. [35 sc]

Motif 5

Make 2 with Yarns A, B, D, and E, and 1 with Yarn C.

Turn after every row. Treat all ch1-sp as sts to be worked.

Row 1 (WS): MR, beg dc, 2dc. [3 dc]

Row 2: (Beg dc, 1dc) in first st, ch1, 2dc in final st. [4 dc, 1 ch1-sp]

Row 3: (Beg dc, 1dc) in first st, ch1, sk1, 1dc, ch1, 2dc in final st. [5 dc, 2 ch1-sp]

Row 4: (Beg dc, 1dc) in first st, ch1, sk1, 3dc, ch1, 2dc in final st. [7 dc, 2 ch1-sp]

Row 5: (Beg dc, 1dc) in first st, [ch1, sk1, 2dc] twice, ch1, 2dc in final st. [8 dc, 3 ch1-sp]

Motif 5

Row 6: (Beg dc, 1dc) in first st, [ch1, sk1, 2dc, ch1, sk1, 1dc] twice, 1dc in same st. [9 dc, 4 ch1-sp]

Row 7: (Beg dc, 1dc) in first st, ch1, sk1, 2dc, ch1, sk1, 1dc in ch-sp, 1dc in each st to next ch-sp, 1dc in ch-sp, ch1, sk1, 2dc, ch1, 2dc in final st. [2 dc inc]

Rows 8–11: Rep Row 7 four times. [19 dc, 4 ch1-sp]

PM in first dc and final dc.

Row 12: Beg dc3tog, ch1, sk1, 2dc, ch1, sk1, 9dc, ch1, sk1, 2dc, ch1, sk1, dc3tog. [2 dc3tog, 13 dc, 4 ch1-sp]

Row 13: Beg dc3tog, ch1, sk1, 2dc, ch1, sk1, 5dc, ch1, sk1, 2dc, ch1, sk1, dc3tog. [2 dc3tog, 9 dc, 4 ch1-sp]

Row 14: Beg dc3tog, ch1, sk1, 2dc, ch1, sk1, 1dc, ch1, sk1, 2dc, ch1, sk1, dc3tog. [2 dc3tog, 5 dc, 4 ch1-sp]

Row 15: Beg dc3tog, ch1, sk1, 3dc, ch1, sk1, dc3tog. [2 dc3tog, 3 dc, 2 ch1-sp]

Row 16: Beg dc3tog, 1dc, dc3tog. [2 dc3tog, 1dc]

Row 17: Beg dc3tog, turn.

Motif Border Rnd: 3sc in dc3tog, working in side of dc sts: [2sc in next sp, 3sc in next sp] twice, 2sc in each of next 2 sp, 3sc in marked st, [2sc in next sp, 3sc in next sp] 4 times, 2sc in each of next 2 sp, 5sc in ring, 2sc in each of next 2 sp, [3sc in next sp, 2sc in next sp] 4 times, 3sc in marked st, 2sc in each of next 2 sp, [3sc in next sp, 2sc in next sp] twice, slst in first sc, fasten off and weave in ends. [90 sc]

Motif 6

Make 1 each with Yarns D and E.

Turn after every row. Treat all ch1-sp as sts to be worked.

Row 1 (WS): MR, beg dc, 1dc. [2 dc]

Row 2: (Beg dc, 1dc) in first st, 1dc. [3 dc]

Row 3: Beg dc, ch1, 2dc in final st. [4 dc]

Row 4: (Beg dc, 1dc) in first st, ch1, sk1, 2dc. [4 dc, 1 ch1-sp]

Row 5: Beg dc, 2dc, ch1, 2dc in final st. [5 dc, 1 ch1-sp]

Row 6: (Beg dc, 1dc) in first st, ch1, sk1, 2dc, ch1, sk1, 1dc. [5 dc, 2 ch1-sp]

Row 7: Beg dc, 1dc, ch1, sk1, 2dc, ch1, 2dc in final st. [6 dc, 2 ch1-sp]

Row 8: (Beg dc, 1dc) in first st, ch1, sk1, 2dc, ch1, sk1, 3dc. [7 dc, 2 ch1-sp]

Row 9: Beg dc, 3dc, ch1, sk1, 2dc, ch1, 2dc in final st. [8 dc, 2 ch1-sp]

Row 10: (Beg dc, 1dc) in first st, ch1, sk1, 2dc, ch1, sk1, 5dc. [9 dc, 2 ch1-sp]

Row 11: Beg dc, 5dc, ch1, sk1, 2dc, ch1, 2dc in final st. PM in final dc. [10 dc, 2 ch1-sp]

Row 12: Beg dc3tog, ch1, sk1, 2dc, ch1, sk1, 5dc. [1 dc3tog, 7 dc, 2 ch1-sp]

Row 13: Beg dc, 2dc, ch1, sk1, 2dc, ch1, sk1, dc3tog. [1 dc3tog, 5dc, 2 ch1-sp]

Row 14: Beg dc3tog, ch1, sk1, 2dc, ch1, sk1, 1dc. [1 dc3tog, 3 dc, 2 ch1-sp]

Row 15: Beg dc, 1dc, ch1, sk1, dc3tog. [1 dc3tog, 2 dc, 1 ch1-sp]

Row 16: Beg dc3tog, 1dc. [1 dc3tog, 1dc]

Row 17: Beg dc2tog, fasten off.

Note: *LH Motif 4 is joined onto work with WS facing.*

Motif Border Row, RH Motif 4: With RS facing, rejoin yarn in starting ring, 3sc in same sp, working in side of dc sts, [2sc in next sp, 3sc in next sp] 4 times, 2sc in each of next 2 sp, 3sc in marked st, 2sc in each of next 2 sp, [3sc in next sp, 2sc in next sp] twice, 2sc in final st, fasten off and weave in ends. [46 sc]

Motif Border Row, LH Motif 4: With WS facing, rejoin yarn in beg dc3tog, 2sc in same st, working in side of dc sts, [2sc in next sp, 3sc in next sp] twice, 2sc in each of next 2 ch-sp, 3sc in marked st, [3sc in next sp, 2sc in next sp] 4 times, 2sc in each of next 2 sp, 3sc in final st, fasten off and weave in ends. [46 sc]

Motif 7

Make 2 with Yarns A and B, and 1 with Yarn C.

Turn after every row. Treat all ch1-sp as sts to be worked.

Row 1 (WS): MR, beg dc, 2dc. [3 dc]

Row 2: (Beg dc, 2dc) in first st, 1dc, 3dc in final st. [7 dc]

Row 3: (Beg dc, 2dc) in first st, ch1, sk1, 3dc, ch1, 3dc in final st. [9 dc, 2 ch1-sp]

Row 4: (Beg dc, 2dc) in first st, [ch1, sk1, 2dc, ch1, sk1, 1dc] twice, 2dc in same st. [11 dc, 4 ch1-sp]

Row 5: (Beg dc, 2dc) in first st, ch1, sk1, 2dc, ch1, sk1, 5dc, ch1, sk1, 2dc, ch1, 3dc in final st. [15 dc, 4 ch1-sp]

Row 6: (Beg dc, 2dc) in first st, ch1, sk1, 2dc, ch1, sk1, 9dc, ch1, sk1, 2dc, ch1, 3dc in final st, do not fasten off. [19 dc, 4 ch1-sp]

Motif Border Row (RS): Working across 2 short sides in sides of dc sts, 2sc in same st, [2sc in next sp, 3sc in next sp] twice, 2sc in each of next 2 sp, 3sc in ring, 2sc in next 2 sp, [3sc in next sp, 2sc in next sp] twice, 2sc in final st, fasten off and weave in ends. [35 sc]

Motif 8 (make 5)

Turn after every row.

Rnd 1 (RS): With Yarn D, MR, beg dc, [ch1, 2dc] 3 times, ch1, 1sc, slst in beg dc, fasten off. [8 dc, 4 ch1-sp]

Rnd 2: Join Yarn C in any ch-sp, beg dc in same sp, [ch2, 2dc in same sp, ch1, 2dc in next ch-sp] 3 times, ch2, 1dc in next ch-sp, slst in beg dc, slst in ch-sp. [16 dc, 4 ch2-sp, 4 ch1-sp]

Rnd 3: Beg dc in same sp, *ch2, 2dc in same sp, [ch1, 2dc in next ch-sp] to next cnr sp, ch1, 2dc in cnr sp; rep from * 3 times more, omitting final dc on last rep, slst in beg dc, fasten off. [8 dc and 4 ch1-sp inc]

Rnd 4: Join Yarn B in any ch2-sp, rep Rnd 3, but do not fasten off, slst in ch-sp. [32 dc, 4 ch2-sp, 12 ch1-sp]

Rnd 5: Rep Rnd 3, fasten off. [40 dc, 4 ch2-sp, 16 ch1-sp]

Rnd 6: Join Yarn A in any ch2-sp, rep Rnd 3, but do not fasten off, slst in ch-sp. [48 dc, 4 ch2-sp, 20 ch1-sp]

Rnd 7: [5sc in ch2-sp, 17sc] 4 times, slst in first sc, fasten off and weave in ends.

Motif 9 (make 5)

Turn after every row.

Rnd 1 (RS): Work as for Motif 8, but do not fasten off, slst in ch-sp.

Rnd 2: Cont with Yarn D, beg dc in same sp and cont rnd as for Motif 6A, fasten off.

Rnd 3: Join Yarn C in any ch2-sp, beg dc in same sp and cont rnd as for Motif 6A, fasten off.

Rnds 4–7: Work as for Motif 6A.

Motif 8

Join the Motifs

With same yarn as either adjacent motif, and following Placement Guide motif layout, Whip-stitch Join adjacent motifs together through both lps with motifs held WS together (see General Techniques: Joining Methods). Weave in all ends.

Make Blanket Border

Rnd 1: Join Yarn A in top right cnr, 3sc in same st, 21sc evenly across each of 5 motifs, 3sc in cnr, 21sc evenly across each of 4 motifs, 34sc across next motif, 3sc in cnr, 21sc evenly across each of 5 motifs, 3sc in cnr, 34sc across next motif, 21sc evenly across each of 4 motifs, slst in first sc.

Rnd 2: With smaller hook, [3sc in cnr st, 1sc in each st to next cnr] 4 times, slst in first sc, fasten off and weave in ends.

Finishing

Weave in any rem ends and block blanket to given measurements and to flatten seams.

Placement Guide

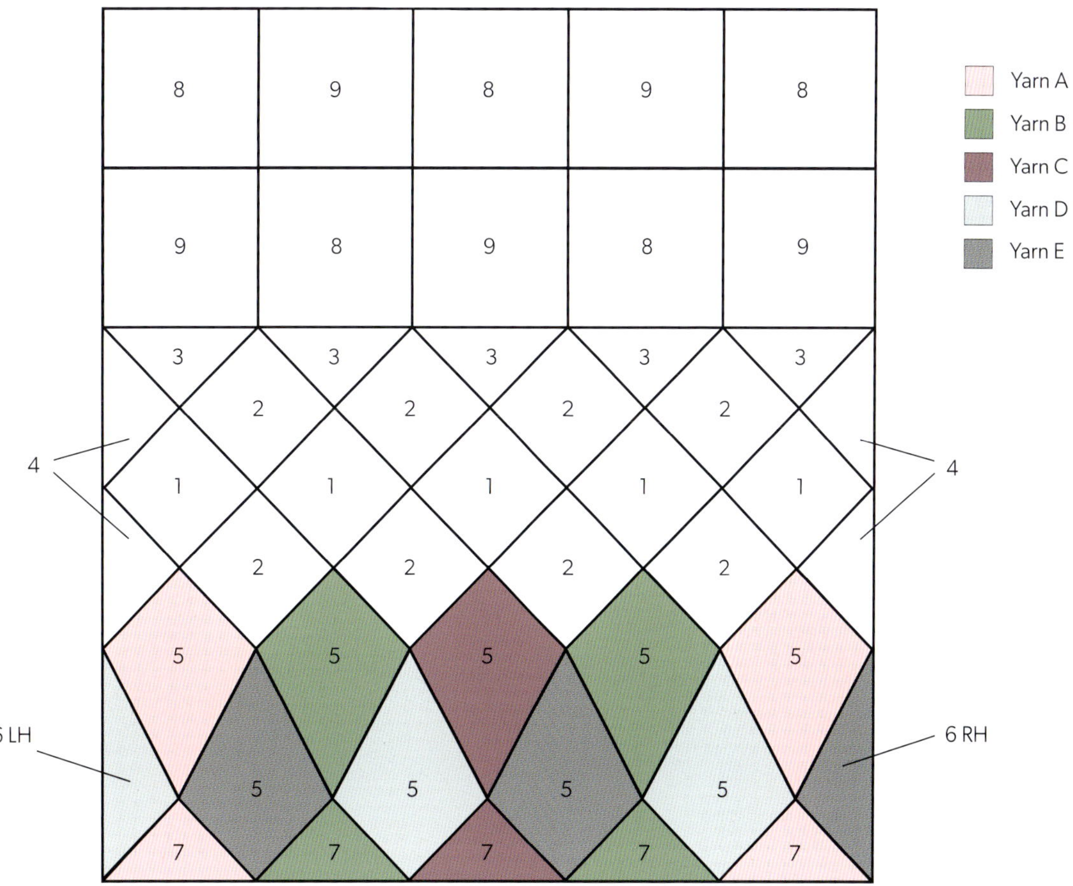

SUNLIGHT VALLEY BLANKET

Inspired by lush fields of sunflowers facing the cascading light of the morning sun, this blanket features rows of large octagon motifs (the sunflowers), dotted with little flower squares in between. The random color selection of the motifs and the addition of sections worked back and forth are a tribute to the natural intertwining of chaos and order in nature. This is the perfect blanket to enjoy in a sunroom or on the patio – anywhere where you are surrounded by nature.

Finished Size

80 x 66in (203 x 167.5cm)

Yarn

Worsted (aran) weight (#4 Medium)

Shown here: Berroco Comfort (50% super fine nylon, 50% super fine acrylic) 100g (210yd/192m) in following colors:

- Yarn A: Pumpkin (9724); 3 balls
- Yarn B: Pretty Pink (9705); 3 balls
- Yarn C: Raspberry Coulis (9717); 3 balls
- Yarn D: Buttercup (9712); 3 balls
- Yarn E: Pimpernel (9742); 3 balls
- Yarn F: Purple (9722); 3 balls
- Yarn G: Lavender Frost (9715); 3 balls
- Yarn H: Pearl (9702) Pearl; 6 balls

Hook

US size G/7 (4.5mm) hook

Gauge (Tension)

18 dc x 9 rows = 4 x 4in (10 x 10cm) using a US G/7 (4.5mm) hook.

Pattern Notes

Motifs are completed then joined with Slip-stitch Join (see General Techniques: Joining Methods), which creates a neat, crisp frame.

Placement Guide shows joining order.

To join new yarns, slst in specified stitch.

Make Blanket Body

For Motifs A–C refer to Motif Color Table for colors to be used.

Motif Color Table

Motifs	C1	C2	C3	C4	C5
A35, B1	E	G	F	B	C
A34, B2	B	D	A	F	E
A10, A20, B8	A	C	D	F	G
A11, A24, B9	F	B	G	A	D
A13, A28, B3	C	A	B	F	G
A12, A32, B4	F	B	D	E	A
A31, A26, C1	A	E	B	D	F
A1, A21, C2	G	F	C	E	A
A15, A27, B10	E	F	D	A	B
A3, A16, B11	C	F	D	G	E
A9, A23, B12	F	B	E	C	A
A8, A14, B13	D	B	G	F	C
A18, A29, B14	G	F	B	D	E
A2, A25, B5	C	E	A	D	B
A6, A33, B6	F	D	G	B	C
A5, A19, B7	A	D	B	G	F
A4, A17	E	A	D	G	B
A7, A22, A30	D	A	E	C	B

Motif A

Motifs A1-A35

Rnd 1 (RS): With C1, MR, beg tr, 23tr, slst in beg tr. [24 tr]

Rnd 2: Beg tr in first st, [ch1, 1tr] 23 times, ch1, slst in beg tr, fasten off. [24 tr, 24 ch1-sp]

Rnd 3: Join C2 in any tr, beg 2dc-cl in same st, [ch2, 2dc-cl in next tr] 23 times, ch2, slst in beg 2dc-cl, fasten off. [24 2dc-cl, 24 ch2-sp]

Rnd 4: Join C3 in any ch-sp, beg 4dc-cl in same sp, [ch3, 4dc-cl in next ch-sp] 23 times, ch3, slst in beg 4dc-cl, fasten off. [24 4dc-cl, 24 ch3-sp]

Rnd 5: Join C4 in any ch-sp, beg dc in same sp, [3dc in same sp, 1dc in next ch-sp] 24 times, omitting final dc on last rep, slst in beg dc. [96 dc]

Rnd 6: Beg dc4tog over first 4 sts, [ch4, dc4tog] 23 times, ch4, slst in beg dc4tog, fasten off. [24 dc4tog, 24 ch4-sp]

Rnd 7: Join C5 in any ch-sp, beg dc in same sp, [ch1, 2dc in same sp, 4dc in next ch-sp, 1dc in next st, 4dc in next ch-sp, 2dc in next ch-sp] 8 times, omitting final dc on eighth rep, slst in beg dc. [104 dc, 8 ch4-sp]

Rnd 8: Beg dc in ch-sp, *ch1, 1dc in same sp, [ch1, sk1, 1dc] 6 times, ch1, 1dc in ch-sp; rep from * 7 times more, omitting final dc on last rep, slst in beg dc. [64 dc, 64 ch1-sp]

Rnd 9: [3sc in cnr sp, 15sc] 8 times, slst in first sc, fasten off and weave in ends. [144 sc]

Motifs B1-B14

Row 1 (RS): With C1, MR, beg tr, 12tr, turn. [13 tr]

Row 2: Beg tr, [ch1, 1tr] 12 times, fasten off, turn. [13 tr, 12 ch-sp]

Row 3: Join C2 in first tr, beg 2dc-cl in same st, [ch2, 2dc-cl in next tr] 12 times, fasten off, do not turn. [13 2dc-cl, 12 ch2-sp]

Join C3 in first st, ready to work another RS row.

Row 4 (RS): Beg dc in first st, ch2, 4dc-cl in next ch-sp, [ch3, 4dc-cl in next ch-sp] 11 times, ch2, 1dc in final st, fasten off, turn. [12 4dc-cl, 2 dc, 11 ch3-sp, 2 ch2-sp]

Row 5: Join C4 in first ch-sp, beg dc in same sp, [2dc in same sp, 2dc in next ch-sp] 12 times, 1dc in same sp, turn. [50 dc]

Row 6: Beg dc3tog over first 3 sts, [ch4, dc4tog] 11 times, ch4, dc3tog, fasten off, do not turn. [11 dc4tog, 2 dc3tog, 12 ch4-sp]

Join C5 in first st, ready to work another RS row.

Row 7 (RS): Beg dc in first st, [4dc in next ch-sp, (2dc, ch1, 2dc) in next ch-sp, 4dc in next ch-sp, 1dc in next st] 4 times, turn. [53 dc, 4 ch1-sp]

Row 8: Beg dc in first st, 1dc, [ch1, sk1, 1dc] twice, ch1, sk1, 1dc in ch-sp, *ch1, 1dc in same sp, [ch1, sk1, 1dc] 6 times, ch1, sk1, 1dc in ch-sp; rep from * twice, ch1, 1dc in same sp, [ch1, sk1, 1dc] 3 times, 1dc, turn. [34 dc, 31 ch1-sp]

Row 9: [8sc, 3sc in cnr sp, 7sc] 4 times, 1sc, fasten off and weave in ends. [73 sc]

Motif C

Motifs C1 and C2

Row 1 (RS): With C1, MR, beg tr, 9tr, turn. [10 tr]

Row 2: Beg tr, [ch1, 1tr] 9 times, fasten off, turn. [10 tr, 9 ch1-sp]

Row 3: Join C2 in first tr, beg 2dc-cl in same st, [ch2, 2dc-cl in next tr] 9 times, fasten off, do not turn. [10 2dc-cl, 9 ch2-sp]

Join C3 in first st, ready to work another RS row.

Row 4 (RS): Beg dc in same st, ch2, 4dc-cl in next ch-sp, [ch3, 4dc-cl in next ch-sp] 8 times, ch2, 1dc in final st, fasten off, turn. [9 4dc-cl, 2 dc, 8 ch3-sp, 2 ch2-sp]

Row 5: Join C4 in first ch-sp, beg dc in same sp, [2dc in same sp, 2dc in next ch-sp] 9 times, 1dc in same sp, turn. [38 dc]

Row 6: Beg dc3tog over first 3 sts, [ch4, dc4tog] 8 times, ch4, dc3tog, fasten off, do not turn. [8 dc4tog, 2 dc3tog, 9 ch4-sp]

Join C5 in first st, ready to work another RS row.

Row 7 (RS): Beg dc in first st, [4dc in next ch-sp, (2dc, ch1, 2dc) in next ch-sp, 4dc in next ch-sp, 1dc in next st] 3 times, turn. [40 dc, 3 ch1-sp]

Row 8: Beg dc in first st, 1dc, [ch1, sk1, 1dc] twice, ch1, sk1, 1dc in ch-sp, *ch1, 1dc in same sp, [ch1, sk1, 1dc] 6 times, ch1, sk1, 1dc in ch-sp; rep from * once more, ch1, 1dc in same sp, [ch1, sk1, 1dc] 3 times, 1dc, turn. [26 dc, 23 ch1-sp]

Row 9: [8sc, 3sc in cnr sp, 7sc] 3 times, 1sc, fasten off and weave in ends. [55 sc]

Motif 4 (make 36)

Make 20 with Yarn H, 2 with Yarns A, B, and E, 4 with Yarns C and G, and 1 with Yarns D and F.

Rnd 1 (RS): MR, 8sc, slst in first sc. [8 sc]

Rnd 2: Beg 2dc-cl, [ch1, 2dc-cl in same st, ch2, pc, ch2, 2dc-cl] 4 times, omitting final 2dc-cl on fourth rep, slst in beg 2dc-cl. [4 pc, 8 2dc-cl, 8 ch2-sp, 4 ch1-sp]

Rnd 3: Slst in ch-sp, [5dc in next ch-sp, picot, 5dc in next ch-sp, slst in next ch-sp] 4 times. [4 picot, 40 dc]

Rnd 4: 1sc in same ch-sp working around slst, [ch4, BPsc around next pc from Rnd 2, ch4, 1sc in next ch1-sp working around slst] 4 times, omitting final sc on fourth rep, slst in first sc. [4 BPsc, 4 sc, 8 ch4-sp]

Rnd 5: Beg dc in first ch-sp, [2dc in same ch-sp, ch1, 3dc in next ch-sp, ch1, (3tr, ch3, 3tr) in next sc, ch1, 1dc in next ch-sp] 4 times, omitting final dc on fourth rep, slst in beg dc. [24 tr, 24 dc, 16 ch3-sp]

Rnd 6: Beg dc in ch-sp, [1dc in backside of picot and same ch-sp together to anchor picot, 1dc in same ch-sp, 3dc in next ch-sp, (3dc, ch1, 3dc) in next ch-sp, 3dc in next ch-sp, 1dc in next ch-sp] 4 times, omitting final dc on fourth rep, slst in beg dc. [60 dc, 4 ch1-sp]

Rnd 7: [9sc, 3sc in cnr sp, 6sc] 4 times, slst in first sc, fasten off and weave in ends. [72 sc]

Motif 4

Motif 5 (make 6)

Make 1 with each of Yarns A–F.

Row 1 (WS): MR, 5sc, turn.

Row 2: Beg pc, [ch2, (2dc-cl, ch1, 2dc-cl) in next st, ch2, pc] twice, fasten off, do not turn. [3 pc, 4 2dc-cl, 4 ch2-sp, 2 ch1-sp]

Row 3 (RS): Slst in first st, beg dc in same st, [picot, 5dc in next ch-sp, slst in next ch-sp, 5dc in next ch-sp] twice, picot, ch1, 1sc in final st, turn. [3 picot, 20 dc]

Row 4: FPsc around pc on Row 2, [ch4, 1sc in next ch1-sp working around slst, ch4, FPsc around next pc from Row 2] twice, turn. [3 FPsc, 2 sc, 4 ch4-sp]

Row 5: Beg dc in first st, ch1, [3dc in next ch-sp, ch1, (3tr, ch3, 3tr) in next sc, ch1, 3dc in next ch-sp, ch1] twice, 1dc in final st, fasten off, do not turn. [12 tr, 14 dc, 7 ch1-sp, 2 ch3-sp]

Row 6 (RS): Slst in first ch-sp, beg dc in backside of picot and same ch-sp together to anchor picot, [1dc in same ch-sp, 3dc in next ch-sp, (3dc, ch1, 3dc) in next ch-sp, 3dc in next ch-sp, 1dc in next ch-sp, 1dc in both picot and same ch-sp together] twice, fasten off, do not turn. [31 dc, 2 ch1-sp]

Row 7 (RS): Slst in first st, [8sc, 3sc in cnr sp, 7sc] twice, 1sc in final st, fasten off and weave in ends. [37 sc]

Motif 6 (make 7)

Make 3 with Yarn H, 2 with Yarn D, and 1 with Yarns E and F.

Row 1 (WS): MR, 5sc, turn. [5 sc]

Row 2: Beg dc, [ch1, 2dc-cl in same st, ch2, pc, ch2, 2dc-cl] twice, ch1, 1dc in same st, fasten off, do not turn. [2 pc, 4 2dc-cl, 2 dc, 4 ch2-sp, 3 ch1-sp]

Row 3 (RS): [Slst in ch1-sp, 5dc in next ch-sp, picot, 5dc in next ch-sp] twice, slst in final ch-sp, turn. [2 picot, 20 dc]

Row 4: 1sc in ch1-sp working around slst, [ch4, FPsc around next pc from Row 2, ch4, 1sc in next ch1-sp working around slst] twice, turn. [2 FPsc, 3 sc, 4 ch4-sp]

Row 5: Beg tr in first sc, ch2, [3tr in same st, ch1, 3dc in next ch-sp, ch1, 3dc in next ch-sp, ch1, 3tr in next sc, ch3] twice, omitting final ch3 on second rep, ch2, 1tr in same st, fasten off, do not turn. [14 tr, 12 dc, 6 ch1-sp, 2 ch2-sp, 1 ch3-sp]

Rejoin yarn in first ch-sp, ready to work another RS row.

Row 6 (RS): Beg dc in first ch-sp, [ch1, 3dc in same sp, 3dc in next ch-sp, 1dc in next ch-sp, 1dc in picot and same ch-sp together, 1dc in same ch-sp, 3dc in each of next 2 ch-sp] twice, ch1, 1dc in same ch-sp, fasten off, do not turn. [32 dc, 3 ch1-sp]

Row 7 (RS): Slst in first ch-sp, [2sc in same sp, 15sc, 1sc in cnr sp] twice, 1sc in same sp, fasten off and weave in ends. [37 sc]

Motif 6

Motif 7 (make 1)

Rows 3, 6, and 7 are worked as RS rows. Rejoin yarn with RS facing.

Row 1 (WS): With Yarn B, MR, 3sc, turn. [3 sc]

Row 2: Beg pc, ch2, (2dc-cl, ch1, 2dc-cl) in next st, ch2, pc, fasten off, do not turn. [2 pc, 2 2dc-cl, 2 ch2-sp, 1 ch1-sp]

Row 3 (RS): Rejoin Yarn B in first st, beg dc in same st, picot, 5dc in next ch-sp, slst in next ch-sp, 5dc in next ch-sp, picot, ch1, 1sc in final st, turn. [2 picot, 12 dc]

Row 4: FPsc around pc on Row 2, ch4, 1sc in next ch1-sp working around slst, ch4, FPsc around next pc from Row 2, turn. [2 FPsc, 1 sc, 2 ch4-sp]

Row 5: Beg dc in first st, ch1, 3dc in next ch-sp, ch1, (3tr, ch3, 3tr) in next sc, ch1, 3dc in next ch-sp, ch1, 1dc in final st, fasten off, do not turn. [6 tr, 8 dc, 4 ch1-sp, 1 ch3-sp]

Row 6 (RS): Rejoin Yarn B in first ch-sp, beg dc in backside of picot and same ch-sp together to anchor picot, 1dc in same ch-sp, 3dc in next ch-sp, (3dc, ch1, 3dc) in next ch-sp, 3dc in next ch-sp, 1dc in next ch-sp, 1dc in picot and same ch-sp together, fasten off, do not turn. [16 dc, 1 ch-sp]

Row 7 (RS): Rejoin Yarn B in first st, 8sc, 3sc in cnr sp, 8sc in final st, fasten off and weave in ends. [19 sc]

Join the Motifs

With Yarn H, join motifs along seams in the order shown on Placement Guide with Slip-stitch Join, working through BLO of both motifs, and holding WS together (see General Techniques: Joining Methods).

Note: *Where a cnr meets 2 motifs, slst twice in that cnr, working in each of 2 motif cnrs to secure both and avoid holes.*

Placement Guide

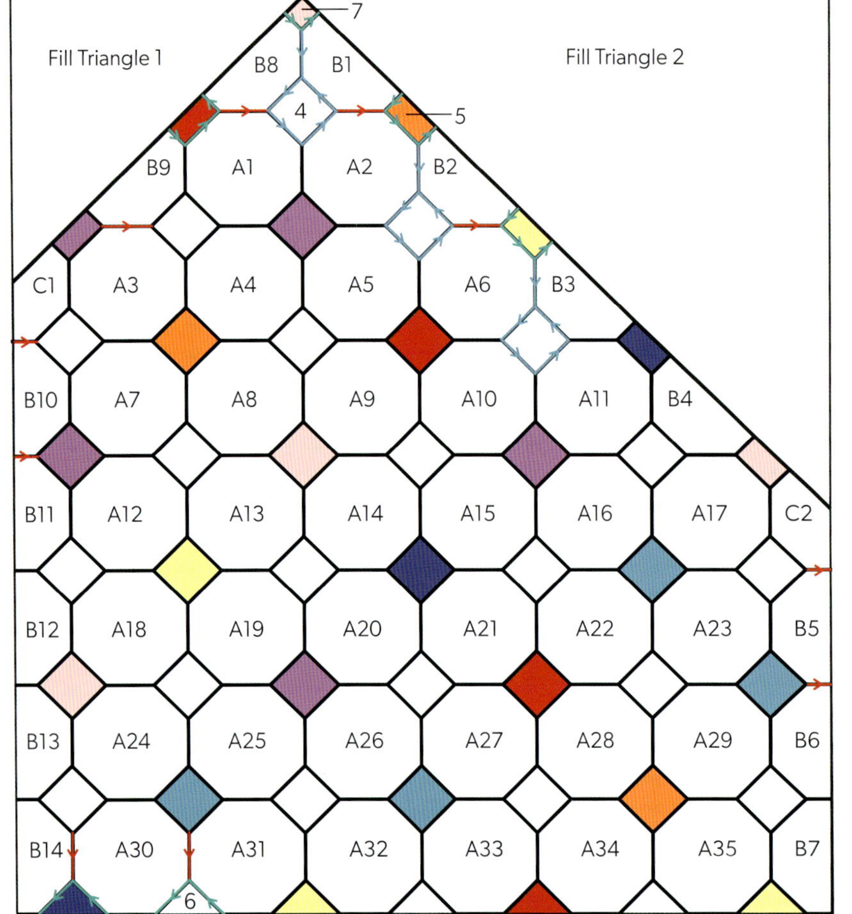

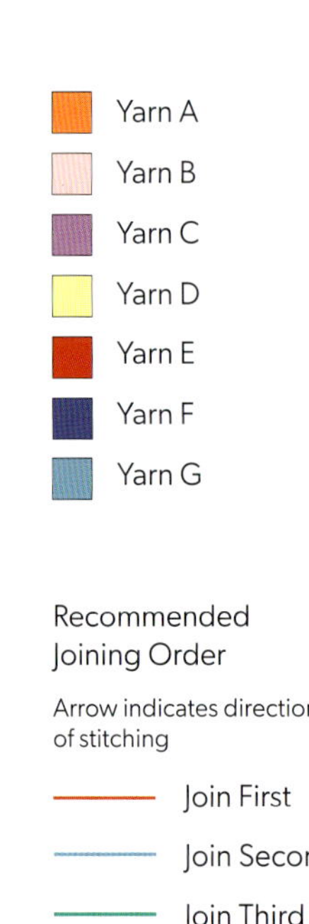

Fill Triangle 1

Rows 10, 11, and 14 are worked as RS rows. Rejoin yarn with RS facing.

Row 1 (RS): Join Yarn H in starting ring of Motif 7, 9sc across Motif 7, [19sc across first half of Motif B, 1sc in starting ring of Motif B, 19sc across second half of Motif B, 17sc across Motif 5 twice, 19sc across Motif C, 1sc in starting ring of Motif C. [141 sc]

Row 2: Beg dc3tog, [ch1, sk1, 1dc] to last 4 sts, ch1, sk1, dc3tog, turn. [2 dc3tog, 67 dc, 68 ch1-sp]

Row 3: Beg dc3tog over first 3 st/sp, [ch2, 1sc in next dc] to last 2 sts, ch2, dc3tog over final 3 st/sp, turn. [2 dc3tog, 65 sc, 66 ch2-sp]

Row 4: Sc2tog over first 2 st/sp, [ch2, 1sc in next ch-sp] to final ch-sp, ch2, sc2tog over final 2 st/sp, turn. [2 sc2tog, 64 sc, 65 ch2-sp]

Row 5: Beg dc3tog over first 3 st/sp, [ch1, 1dc in next ch-sp] to final 2 sts, ch1, dc3tog over final 3 st/sp, turn. [2 dc3tog, 63 dc, 64 ch1-sp]

Row 6: Sc2tog, 1sc in each st/sp across to final ch-sp, sc2tog over final 2 st/sp, fasten off, turn. [2 sc2tog, 125 sc]

Row 7: Join Yarn A in first st, beg dc3tog over first 3 sts, 1dc in all sts to final 3 sts, dc3tog over final 3 sts, turn. [2 dc3tog, 121 dc]

Row 8: Beg tr4tog over first 4 sts, [ch1, sk1, 1tr] 12 times, ch1, sk1, tr4tog over final 4 sts, fasten off, turn. [2 tr4tog, 57 tr, 58 ch1-sp]

Row 9: Join Yarn D in first st, beg dc3tog over first 3 st/sp, [ch1, 2dc-cl in next st] to final 2 ch-sp, ch1, sk 1 ch-sp, dc3tog over final 3 st/sp, fasten off, do not turn. [2 dc3tog, 55 2dc-cl, 56 ch1-sp]

Row 10 (RS): Join Yarn F in first st, beg dc3tog over first 3 st/sp, [ch1, 3dc-cl in next ch-sp] to final 2 sts, ch1, dc3tog over final 3 st/sp, fasten off, do not turn. [2 dc3tog, 54 3dc-cl, 55 ch1-sp]

Row 11 (RS): Join Yarn C in first st, beg tr4tog over first 4 st/sp, [sk 1 ch-sp, (2tr-cl, ch2, 2tr-cl) in next ch-sp] to final 3 ch-sp, sk 1 ch-sp, tr4tog over final 4 st/sp, fasten off, turn. [2 tr4tog, 50 2tr-cl, 25 ch-sp]

Row 12: Join Yarn E in first st, beg dc in first st, 4dc in each ch-sp across, 1dc in final st, turn. [102 dc]

Row 13: Beg dc in first st, [dc4tog, ch3] to final st, 1dc, fasten off, do not turn. [25 dc4tog, 2 dc, 24 ch3-sp]

Row 14 (RS): Join Yarn H in first st, sc2tog, 4sc in each ch-sp to final ch-sp, 3sc in final ch-sp, sc2tog, turn. [2 sc2tog, 95 sc]

Rows 15–27: Rep Rows 2–14 once more, using Yarns H, G, A, E, B, C, H. [2 sc2tog, 51 sc]

Rows 28–40: Rep Rows 2–14 once more, using Yarns H, F, B, D, E, G, H. [2 sc2tog, 7 sc]

Row 41 (WS): Beg dc3tog, ch1, sk1, 1dc, ch1, sk1, dc3tog, turn. [2 dc3tog, 1 dc, 2 ch1-sp]

Row 42: Beg sc5tog, fasten off and weave in ends.

Fill Triangle 2

Row 1 (RS): Join Yarn H in starting ring of Motif C2, 1sc in ring, 19sc across Motif C2, [17sc across Motif 5, 19sc across first half of Motif B, 1sc in starting ring of Motif B, 19sc across second half of Motif B] 4 times, 9sc across Motif 7. [253 sc]

Rows 2–14: Rep Rows 2–14 of Fill Triangle 1 using Yarns H, A, D, F, C, E, H. [2 sc2tog, 207 sc]

Rows 15–27: As Rows 2–14 using Yarns H G, A, E, B, C, H. [2 sc2tog, 159 sc]

Rows 28–40: As Rows 2–14 using Yarns H, F, B, D, E, G, H. [2 sc2tog, 115 sc]

Rows 41–53: As Rows 2–14 using Yarns H, G, A, E, B, C, H. [2 sc2tog, 71 sc]

Rows 54–66: As Rows 2–14 using Yarns H, A, D, F, C, E, H. [2 sc2tog, 27 sc]

Rows 67–71: Cont with Yarn H for rem of Fill Triangle, rep Rows 2–6 once more. [2 sc2tog, 17 sc]

Rows 72–74: Rep Rows 2–4 once more. [2 sc2tog, 3 sc, 4 ch2-sp]

Row 75: Beg dc3tog over first 3 sts/sps, [ch1, 1dc in next ch-sp] twice, ch1, dc3tog over final 3 sts/sps. [2 dc3tog, 2dc, 3 ch-sp]

Row 76: Beg dc7tog over all sts/sps. Fasten off, weave in ends.

Make Blanket Border

Rnd 1: Join Yarn H in top right cnr (corner of Fill Triangle 2), [3sc in cnr, 272sc, 3sc in cnr, 311sc] twice, slst in first sc.

Rnd 2: *(1sc, ch3, 1sc) in cnr, [sk2, (1sc, ch3, 1sc) in next st] until 2 sts before cnr st, sk2; rep from * 3 times more, slst in first sc. Fasten off and weave in ends.

Finishing

Weave in any rem ends and block blanket to given measurements and to open up lacy features.

JEWELS AND GEMS BLANKET

For this stunning and stately piece, I drew inspiration from faceted gems and jewelry. Incorporating these visuals into the design, I mixed some unique geometric motifs and the result is a blanket that you can pass down through the generations as an heirloom. Perfect as a bedspread, this pattern will be outstanding with any decor.

Finished Size

75 x 75in (190.5 x 190.5cm)

Yarn

Worsted (aran) weight (#4 Medium)

Shown here: Knit Picks Brava Worsted/ Brava Speckle/Brava Stripe (100% premium acrylic) 100g (218yd/200m); 1 ball each in following colors, unless otherwise specified:

- Yarn A: Solstice Heather; 2 balls
- Yarn B: Sky
- Yarn C: Clarity
- Yarn D: Snow Day Speckle
- Yarn E: Paprika
- Yarn F: Canary
- Yarn G: Custard
- Yarn H: Gingerbread
- Yarn I: Brindle; 2 balls
- Yarn J: Just Peachy Speckle
- Yarn K: White; 6 balls
- Yarn L: Twilight (Stripe)
- Yarn M: Spice Cabinet (Stripe)
- Yarn N: Buttercream (Stripe)

Hook

- US size H/8 (5mm) hook

Gauge (Tension)

18 dc x 9 rows = 4 x 4in (10 x 10cm) using a US I/9 (5.5mm) hook.

Pattern Notes

To join new yarns, slst in specified stitch.

Make Blanket Body

Motif 1 (make 30)

	C1	C2	C3	C4	C5
1A x 8	G	F	E	J	H
1B x 8	C	B	A	D	J
1C x 4	C	B	L	M	A
1D x 4	N	C	N	J	H
1E x 4	G	F	M	L	H
1F x 2	N	G	N	M	J

Rnd 1: With C1, MR, beg 2tr-cl [ch1, 2tr-cl] 7 times, ch1, slst in beg 2tr-cl. [8 2tr-cl, 8 ch1-sp]

Rnd 2: Beg 3tr-cl in first ch-sp, [ch2, 3tr-cl in same sp, ch2, 3tr-cl in next ch-sp] 8 times, omitting final 3tr-cl on eighth rep, slst in beg 3tr-cl, fasten off. [16 3tr-cl, 16 ch2-sp]

Rnd 3: Join C2 in first ch-sp, beg dc in same sp, [3dc in same sp, ch1, 1dc in next ch-sp] 16 times, omitting final dc on 16th rep, slst in beg dc. [64 dc, 16 ch1-sp]

Rnd 4: Beg dc4tog, [ch4, sk 1 ch-sp, dc4tog] 16 times, omitting final dc4tog on 16th rep, slst in first dc4tog, fasten off. [16 dc4tog, 16 ch4-sp]

Rnd 5: Join C3 in first ch-sp, beg dc in same sp, [4dc in same sp, ch1, 1dc in next ch-sp] 16 times, omitting final dc on 16th rep, slst in beg dc. [80 dc, 16 ch1-sp]

Rnd 6: Slst in 2 sts, 1sc in same st, [ch3, 1sc in next ch-sp, ch3, sk2, 1sc] 16 times, omitting final sc on 16th rep, slst in first sc. [32 sc, 32 ch3-sp]

Rnd 7: [1sc in ch-sp, ch3] 32 times, slst in first sc, fasten off. [32 sc, 32 ch3-sp]

Rnd 8: Join C4 in any ch-sp, beg dc in same sp, [ch1, 2dc in same sp, 3dc in each of next 3 ch-sp, 2dc in next ch-sp] 8 times, omitting final dc on eighth rep, slst in beg dc. [104 dc, 8 ch1-sp]

Rnd 9: Beg dc in first ch-sp, *ch1, 1dc in same sp, [ch1, sk1, 1dc] 6 times, ch1, 1dc in next ch-sp; rep from * 7 times more, omitting final dc on last rep, slst in beg dc, fasten off. [64 dc, 64 ch1-sp]

Rnd 10: Join C5 in first cnr ch-sp, [3sc in cnr sp, sk1, 1sc in each st/sp to last st before cnr sp, sk1] 8 times, slst in first sc, fasten off and weave in ends. [128 sc]

Motif 1

Motif 1 Chart

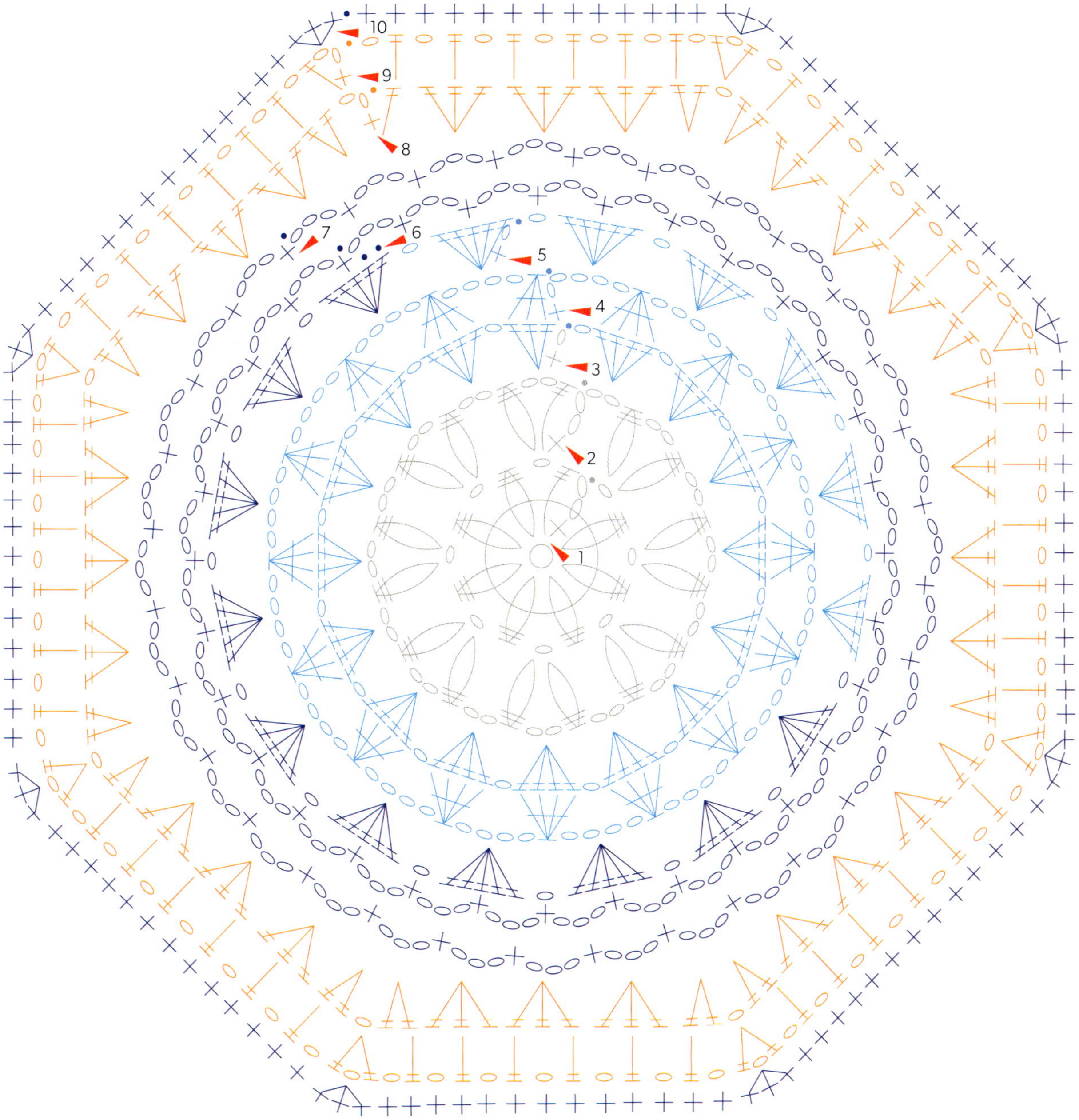

Motif 2

Make 10 with Yarn I. Turn after every row.

Make 2 with Yarn H. Turn after every row.

Row 1 (RS): MR, [1sc, ch1] twice, 1sc, PM in starting ring. [3 sc, 2 ch1-sp]

Row 2: (1sc, ch1, 1sc) in first ch-sp, ch1, (1sc, ch1, 1sc) in final ch-sp. [4 sc, 3 ch1-sp]

Row 3: (1sc, ch1, 1sc) in first ch-sp, ch1, 1sc in next ch-sp, ch1, (1sc, ch1, 1sc) in final ch-sp. [5 sc, 4 ch1-sp]

Row 4: (1sc, ch1, 1sc) in first ch-sp, [ch1, 1sc in next ch-sp] to final ch-sp, ch1, (1sc, ch1, 1sc) in final ch-sp. [1 sc, 1 ch1-sp inc]

Rows 5–11: Rep Row 4 another 7 times. [13 sc, 12 ch1-sp]

Rows 12–27: [ch1, 1sc in next ch-sp] to end. [12 sc, 12 ch1-sp]

PM at beg and end of Rows 12 and 27.

Rows 28–38: [1sc in next ch-sp, ch1] to final ch-sp, 1sc in final ch-sp. [2 sc, 1 ch1-sp]

Row 39: 1sc in ch-sp, PM, do not turn.

***Note:** First motif is at top left of blanket and worked complete without joining. Join rem motifs as instructed, working in rows across and down the blanket.*

Motif Border Rnd: [3sc in marked st, 13sc evenly to next marked st] 6 times, slst in first sc, fasten off and weave in ends. [96 sc]

Motif 2 Chart

Motif 2

Motif 3

Make 30 with Yarn K.

Rnd 1: MR, beg dc, [ch1, 3dc] 3 times, ch1, 2dc, slst in beg dc. [12 dc, 4 ch1-sp]

Rnd 2: Beg dc in ch-sp, [ch1, 3dc in same sp, ch1, 3dc in next ch-sp] 4 times, omitting final dc on fourth rep, slst in beg dc. [24 dc, 8 ch1-sp]

Rnd 3: 3sc in first ch, [7sc, 5sc in next ch] 3 times, 7sc, 2sc in same space as first 3sc. [48 sc]

Rnd 4: Beg dc in cnr st, *ch1, 2dc in same st, [sk2, 3dc in next st] 3 times, sk2, 2dc in next st]; rep from * 3 times more, omitting final dc on last rep, slst in beg dc. [52 dc, 4 ch1-sp]

Rnd 5: [3sc in cnr sp, 13sc] 4 times, slst in first sc, fasten off and weave in ends. [64 sc]

Motif 4

Make 22 with Yarn K. Turn after every row.

Row 1: MR, beg dc, [ch1, 3dc] twice, ch1, 1dc. [8 dc, 3 ch1-sp]

Row 2: Beg dc in ch-sp, [ch1, 3dc in same sp, ch1, 3dc in next ch-sp] twice, ch1, 1dc in same sp. [14 dc, 5 ch1-sp]

Row 3: 2sc in first ch-sp, 7sc, 5sc in cnr sp, 7sc, 3sc in final sp. [24 sc]

Row 4: Beg dc in cnr st, *ch1, 2dc in same st, [sk2, 3dc in next st] 3 times, sk2, 2dc in next st; rep from * once more, ch1, 1dc in same st. [28 dc, 3 ch1-sp]

Row 5: 2sc in first ch-sp, 13sc, 3sc in cnr sp, 13sc, 2sc in final ch-sp, fasten off and weave in ends. [33 sc]

Motif 3

Motif 3 Chart

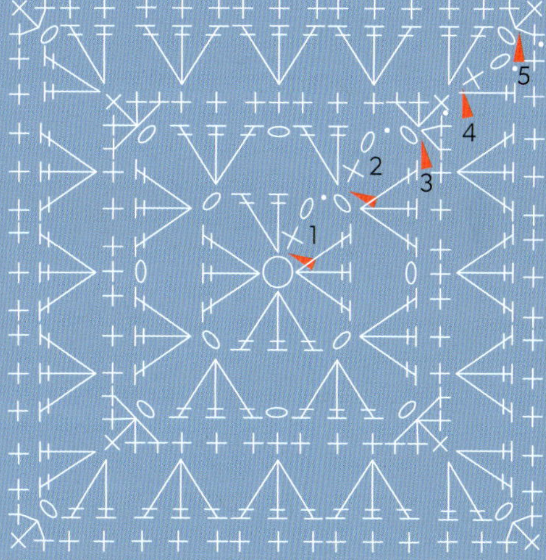

Motif 4 Chart

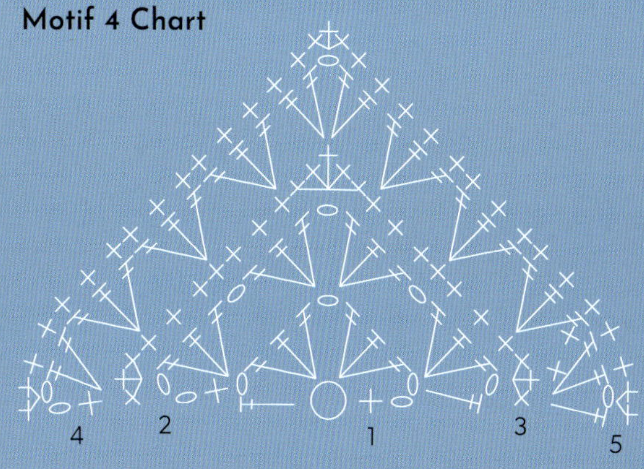

Motif 5

Make 4 with Yarn K. Turn after every row.

Row 1: MR, beg dc, ch1, 3dc, ch1, 1dc. [5 dc, 2 ch1-sp]

Row 2: Beg dc in ch-sp, ch1, 3dc in same sp, ch1, (3dc, ch1, 1dc) in next ch-sp. [8 dc, 3 ch1-sp]

Row 3: 3sc in first ch-sp, 7sc, 3sc in final sp. [13 sc]

Row 4: Beg dc in cnr st, ch1, 2dc in same st, [sk2, 3dc in next st] 3 times, sk2, (2dc, ch1, 1dc) in final st. [15 dc, 2 ch1-sp]

Row 5: 2sc in first ch-sp, 13sc, 2sc in final ch-sp, fasten off and weave in ends. [17 sc]

Motif 5 Chart

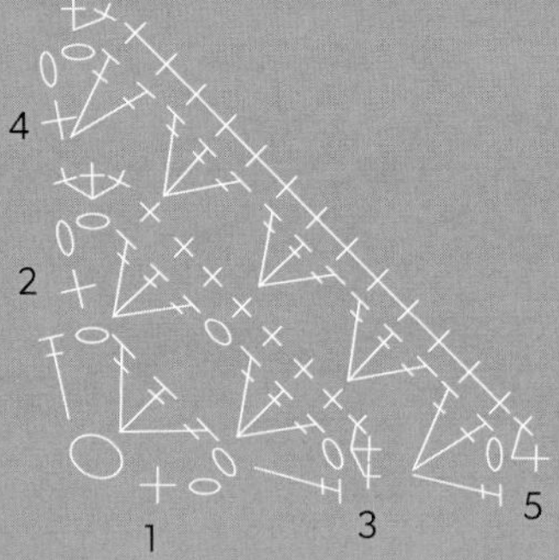

Join the Motifs

With Yarn A, following Placement Guide, join adjacent motifs together using Slip-stitch Join (see General Techniques: Joining Methods) through both lps with motifs held WS together, first joining all of Motifs 1 and 2, then joining on Motifs 3, 4, and 5. Weave in all ends.

Placement Guide

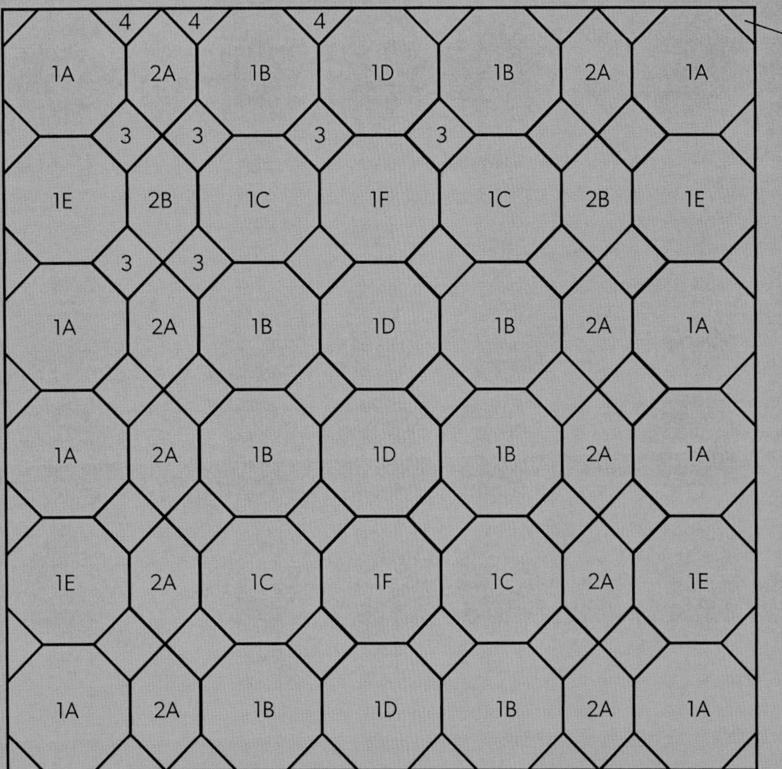

Make Blanket Border

Rnd 1: With Yarn A, slst in top right cnr of blanket, [3sc in cnr st, sc evenly across side – so make 9sc across Motif 5, 16sc across Motif 1, and 19sc across Motif 4] 4 times, slst in first sc.

Rnd 2: *[1sc, ch3] 3 times in cnr st, 1sc in same st, [sk2, (1sc, ch3, 1sc) in next st] across to next cnr st, rep from * 3 times more, slst in first sc, fasten off and weave in ends.

Rnd 3: [3sc in cnr sp, 1sc in all st/sp to next cnr] 4 times, slst in first sc.

Rnd 4: Beg dc in cnr st, *(3dc, picot, 4dc) in same st, [sk2, (2dc, picot, 2dc) in next st] to next cnr, 1dc in cnr st, rep from * 3 times more, omitting final dc on last rep, slst in beg dc, fasten off and weave in ends.

Finishing

Weave in any rem ends and block blanket to given measurements and to flatten seams.

COZY MEADOW BLANKET

A combination of plain and floral hexagon motifs worked up in a bouquet of lush colors makes this the perfect blanket for getting cozy by the fire or while reading a book in your favorite chair. Snuggle under a meadow of flowers and admire the subtle textures of this low-effort, high-style make.

Finished Size

48 x 38in (122 x 96.5cm)

Yarn

Light worsted (DK) weight (#3 Light)

Shown here: Scheepjes Terrazzo Colour Pack (70% recycled mulesing-free wool, 30% recycled viscose) 10g (38yd/35m):

- 1 pack of 60 10g balls

Scheepjes Terrazzo (70% recycled mulesing-free wool, 30% recycled viscose) 50g (175yd/160m):

- Yarn A: 734 Opale; 1 ball

Hook

- US size G/6 (4mm) hook

Gauge (Tension)

20 dc x 8 rows = 4 x 4in (10 x 10cm) using a US G/6 (4mm) hook.

Pattern Notes

Motifs are worked in order and color shown in Placement Guide.

Motif 1 is completed without joining. All other motifs are joined as you go on final round using PLT Join for Hexagons (see General Techniques: Joining Methods).

For most colors, one Flower Motif and one Granny Hexagon Motif are made from each 10g ball. Edge Motif and remainder of blanket are worked from ball leftovers.

Keep each color together with its ball band for easy identification, and save all leftovers to use in blanket border.

To join new yarns, slst in specified stitch.

Make Blanket Body

Follow Placement Guide to see which color to use and whether to make a Flower Motif or a Granny Hexagon Motif as you create blanket body from bottom to top. Center motifs are worked and joined as you go, and then Edge Motifs are worked and joined onto the main blanket.

Placement Guide

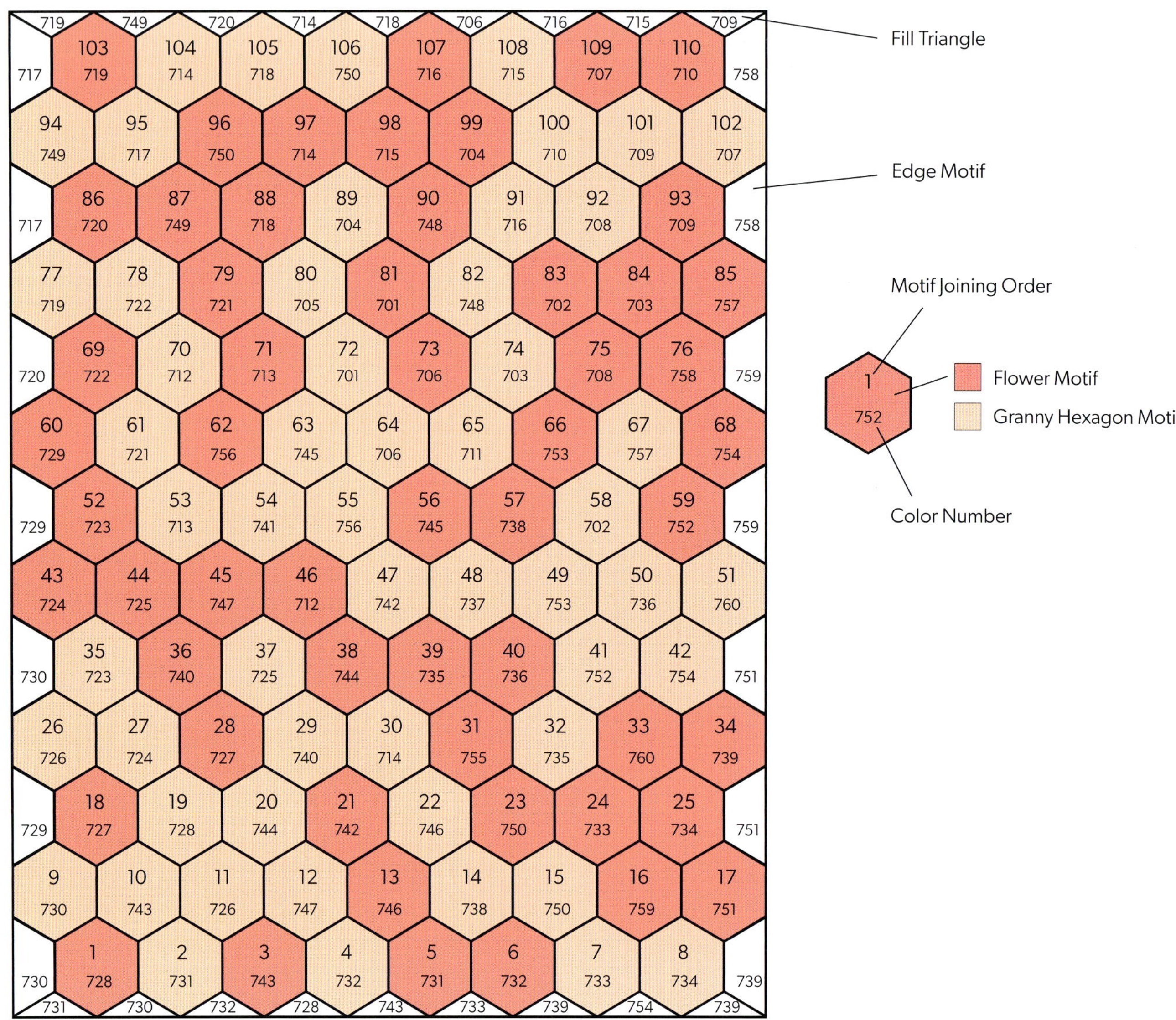

Flower Motif

Rnd 1: MR, beg 2dc-cl, [ch2, 2dc-cl] 5 times, ch2, slst in beg 2dc-cl. [6 2dc-cl, 6 ch2-sp]

Rnd 2: Beg 3dc-cl in ch-sp, [picot, 3dc-cl in same sp, ch1, 3dc-cl in next ch-sp] 6 times, omitting final 3dc-cl on sixth rep, slst in beg 3dc-cl. [6 picot, 12 3dc-cl, 6 ch1-sp]

Rnd 3: Release lp from hook, insert hook from back to front through beg 3dc-cl, pull lp to back of work elongating lp slightly, 1sc in beg 2dc-cl of Rnd 1, [ch4, 1sc in next 2dc-cl of Rnd 1] 6 times, omitting final sc on sixth rep, slst in first sc. [6 sc, 6 ch4-sp]

Rnd 4: Beg 2dc-cl in ch-sp, [(ch2, 3dc-cl, picot, 3dc-cl, ch2, 2dc-cl) in same sp, 1sc in ch1-sp of Rnd 2, 2dc-cl in next ch-sp] 6 times, omitting final 2dc-cl on sixth rep, slst in beg 2dc-cl. [6 picot, 12 3dc-cl, 12 2dc-cl, 6 sc, 12 ch2-sp]

Rnd 5: Pull working lp through beg 2dc-cl as before, ch3 (does not count as a st), [1sc between next 2 3dc-cl sts, working around ch4-sp of Rnd 3, ch5] 6 times, slst in first sc. [6 sc, 6 ch5-sp]

Rnd 6: Slst in next 3 ch, beg dc in ch-sp, [ch1, 3dc in same sp, 1sc in back of sc used to close picot of Rnd 4, 3dc in next ch-sp] 6 times, omitting final dc on sixth rep, slst in beg dc, do not fasten off. [36 dc, 6 sc, 6 ch1-sp]

Cont to Joining Center Motifs and work Joining Rnd according to Motif number.

Flower Motif

Granny Hexagon Motif

Rnd 1: MR, beg 2dc-cl, [ch2, 2dc-cl] 5 times, ch2, slst in beg 2dc-cl. [6 2dc-cl, 6 ch2-sp]

Rnd 2: Slst in 1 ch, beg dc in ch-sp, [ch2, 2dc in same sp, 2dc in next ch-sp] 6 times, omitting final dc on sixth rep, slst in beg dc. [24 dc, 6 ch2-sp]

Rnd 3: Slst in 1 ch, beg dc in ch-sp, [ch2, 1dc in same sp, 2dc, ch1, 2dc, 1dc in next sp] 6 times, omitting final dc on sixth rep, slst in beg dc, do not fasten off. [36 dc, 6 ch2-sp, 6 ch1-sp]

Cont to Joining Motif Center section and work Joining Rnd according to Motif number.

Granny Hexagon Motif

Joining Center Motifs

Joining Rnd will change depending on whether 1, 2, or 3 sides are joined. Locate number of motif you are working and follow instructions. For example, if you are on Motif 26, work instructions under "1 Side: Motifs 2–9, 26, 43, 60, 77, and 94" section. For PLT Join, see General Techniques: Joining Methods.

MOTIF 1 (WORKED WITHOUT JOINING)
Joining Rnd: [3sc in ch-sp, 7sc] 6 times, slst in first sc, fasten off. [60 sc]

1 SIDE: MOTIFS 2–9, 26, 43, 60, 77, AND 94
Joining Rnd: 3sc in ch-sp, 7sc, 2sc in next ch-sp, PLT, 1sc in same sp, [PLT, 1sc] 7 times, PLT, 1sc in next ch-sp, PLT, 2sc in same sp, [7sc, 3sc in next ch-sp] 3 times, 7sc, slst in first sc, fasten off. [60 sc]

3 SIDES: MOTIFS 10-16, 19-25, 27-33, 36-42, 44-50, 53-59, 61-67, 70-76, 78-84, 87-93, 95-101, AND 104-110
Joining Rnd: 3sc in ch-sp, 7sc, 2sc in next ch-sp, PLT, *1sc in same sp, [PLT, 1sc] 7 times, PLT, 1sc in next ch-sp, PLT, 1sc in same sp, PLT in cnr sc of next motif; rep from * once more, 1sc in same sp, [PLT, 1sc] 7 times across next motif, PLT, 1sc in next ch-sp, PLT, 2sc in same sp, 7sc, 3sc in next ch-sp, 7sc, slst in first sc, fasten off. [60 sc]

2 SIDES: MOTIFS 17, 18, 34, 35, 51, 52, 68, 69, 85, 86, 102 AND 103
Joining Rnd: 3sc in ch-sp, 7sc, 2sc in next ch-sp, PLT, 1sc in same sp, [PLT, 1sc] 7 times, PLT, 1sc in next ch-sp, PLT, 1sc in same sp, PLT in cnr sc of next motif, 1sc in same sp, [PLT, 1sc] 7 times across next motif, PLT, 1sc in next ch-sp, PLT, 2sc in same sp, [7sc, 3sc in ch-sp] twice, 7sc, slst in first sc, fasten off. [60 sc]

Edge Motif

Row 1 (RS): MR, beg dc, [ch2, 2dc-cl] 3 times, ch2, 1dc, turn. [3 2dc-cl, 2 dc, 4 ch2-sp]

Row 2: Beg dc in ch-sp, [ch2, 2dc in same sp, 2dc in next ch-sp] 3 times, ch2, 1dc in same sp. [14 dc, 4 ch2-sp]

Row 3: Beg dc in ch-sp, [ch2, 1dc in same sp, 2dc, ch1, 2dc, 1dc in next ch-sp] 3 times, ch2, 1dc in same sp, fasten off. [20 dc, 7 ch2-sp]

Cont to Joining Edge Motifs, rejoining yarn in starting st of Joining Rnd.

Edge Motif

Joining Edge Motifs

Joining Rnd will add Edge Motif onto blanket as shown on Placement Guide. Note that you will join first 2 sides, second 2 sides, or all 3 sides, depending where on blanket motif is being joined.

Joining Rnd (joining first 2 sides): 1sc in cnr sp, PLT in cnr sc where Edge Motif will join, 1sc in same sp on motif in progress, PLT, [1sc in next st/sp, PLT] 7 times, 1sc in next sp, PLT, 1sc in same sp, PLT in cnr sc of next motif, 1sc in same sp, PLT, [1sc, PLT] 7 times, 1sc in next sp, PLT, 2sc in same sp, 7sc, 2sc in final sp, fasten off. [31 sc]

Joining Rnd (joining second 2 sides): 2sc in cnr sp, 7sc, 2sc in next sp, PLT in cnr sc where Edge Motif will join, 1sc in same sp, PLT, [1sc, PLT] 7 times, 1sc in next sp, PLT, 1sc in same sp, PLT in cnr sc of next motif, 1sc in same sp, PLT, [1sc, PLT] 7 times, 1sc in next sp, PLT, 1sc in same sp, fasten off. [31 sc]

Joining Rnd (joining all 3 sides): 1sc in cnr sp, PLT in cnr sc where Edge Motif will join, 1sc in same sp on motif in progress, PLT, [1sc in next st/sp, PLT] 7 times, 1sc in next sp, PLT, 1sc in same sp, PLT in cnr of next motif, 1sc in same sp, PLT, [1sc, PLT] 7 times, 1sc in next sp, PLT, 1sc in same sp, PLT in cnr of next motif, 1sc in same sp, PLT, [1sc, PLT] 7 times, 1sc in next sp, PLT, 1sc in same sp, fasten off. [31 sc]

Cont to Fill Triangles.

Fill Triangles

Each triangle gap is filled separately with color shown in Placement Guide.

Row 1 (RS): Holding panel with RS facing, join yarn in second dc of Motif 103, 1sc in same st, 1sc, 2hdc, 4dc, dc4tog, 4dc, 2hdc, 2sc, turn. [1 dc4tog, 8 dc, 4 hdc, 4 sc]

Row 2: Slst in first 2 sts, 2sc, 2hdc, 1dc, dc3tog, 1dc, 2hdc, 2sc, turn. [1 dc3tog, 2 dc, 4 hdc, 4 sc]

Row 3: Slst in first 2 sts, 2sc, sc3tog, 2sc, fasten off. [1 sc3tog, 4 sc]

Fill rem 8 triangle gaps across top edge of blanket in this same manner with colors shown on Placement Guide, then rotate panel to fill 9 triangle gaps across bottom edge of blanket.

Weave in all ends. Cont to Blanket Border.

Make Blanket Border

Rnd 1: Join Yarn A in top left cnr of blanket, *3sc in cnr st, 18sc across Edge Motif, [9sc across Flower/ Granny Hexagon Motif, 19sc across Edge Motif] to final Edge Motif, 18sc across Edge Motif, 3sc in cnr st, [15sc across fill triangle, 1sc in skipped cnr st on hexagon] to next cnr st; rep from * once more, slst in first sc.

Rnd 2: Beg dc in cnr st, *ch2, 1dc in same st, [ch1, sk1, 1dc] to next cnr, ch1, 1dc in cnr st; rep from * 3 times more, omitting final dc on last rep, slst in beg dc.

Note: *Tr sts on Rnd 3 make tiny bobbles on the RS of the work.*

Rnd 3: *[1sc, 1tr] twice in ch2-sp, 1sc in same sp, [1tr in next st, 1sc in next ch-sp] to last st before cnr sp, 1tr in next st, rep from * 3 times more, slst in first sc, fasten off and weave in ends.

Finishing

Weave in any rem ends and block blanket to given measurements and to flatten seams.

Fill Triangle

STREETSCAPE BLANKET

This project incorporates two lines using different yarns of the same thickness for a lesson in color, creativity, and depth. Included in the design are a mix of familiar stitches and some new techniques to learn, for a relaxing crafting experience. Inspired by the bustling sidewalks and brightly-colored landscapes of the inner city, this piece has an Art Deco color-block effect that is perfect for the modern living space.

Finished Size

65 x 57in (165 x 145cm)

Yarn

Worsted (aran) weight (#4 Medium)

Shown here: Scheepjes Cahlista (100% premium-blend cotton) 50g (93yd/85m); 2 balls each in following colors, unless otherwise specified:

- Yarn A: 514 Jade
- Yarn B: 385 Crystalline
- Yarn C: 244 Spruce
- Yarn D: 400 Petrol Blue
- Yarn E: 394 Shadow Purple
- Yarn F: 517 Ruby
- Yarn G: 258 Rosewood
- Yarn H: 249 Saffron
- Yarn I: 124 Ultramarine; 1 ball
- Yarn J: 521 Deep Violet; 1 ball
- Yarn K: 398 Colonial Rose; 1 ball
- Yarn L: 106 Snow White; 18 balls

Scheepjes SKIES Heavy (100% premium-blend cotton), 100g (186yd/170m); 1 hank each in following colors:

- Yarn M: 104 Altostratus
- Yarn N: 103 Altocumulus
- Yarn O: 102 Cumulus
- Yarn P: 100 Cirrocumulus

Hook

- US size G/6 (4mm) hook

Gauge (Tension)

16 dc x 8 rows = 4 x 4in (10 x 10cm) using a US G/6 (4mm) hook.

Pattern Notes

Center Panel motifs are joined as you go using PLT Join for Hexagons. Border Panel motifs are completed then joined foll Placement Guide using Slip-stitch Join with BLO and motifs held RS together (see General Techniques: Joining Methods).

To join new yarns, slst in specified stitch.

Make Blanket Body

This blanket is worked in two sections – the Center Panel and the Border Panel. Each section is joined as you go according to the Placement Guide.

Placement Guide

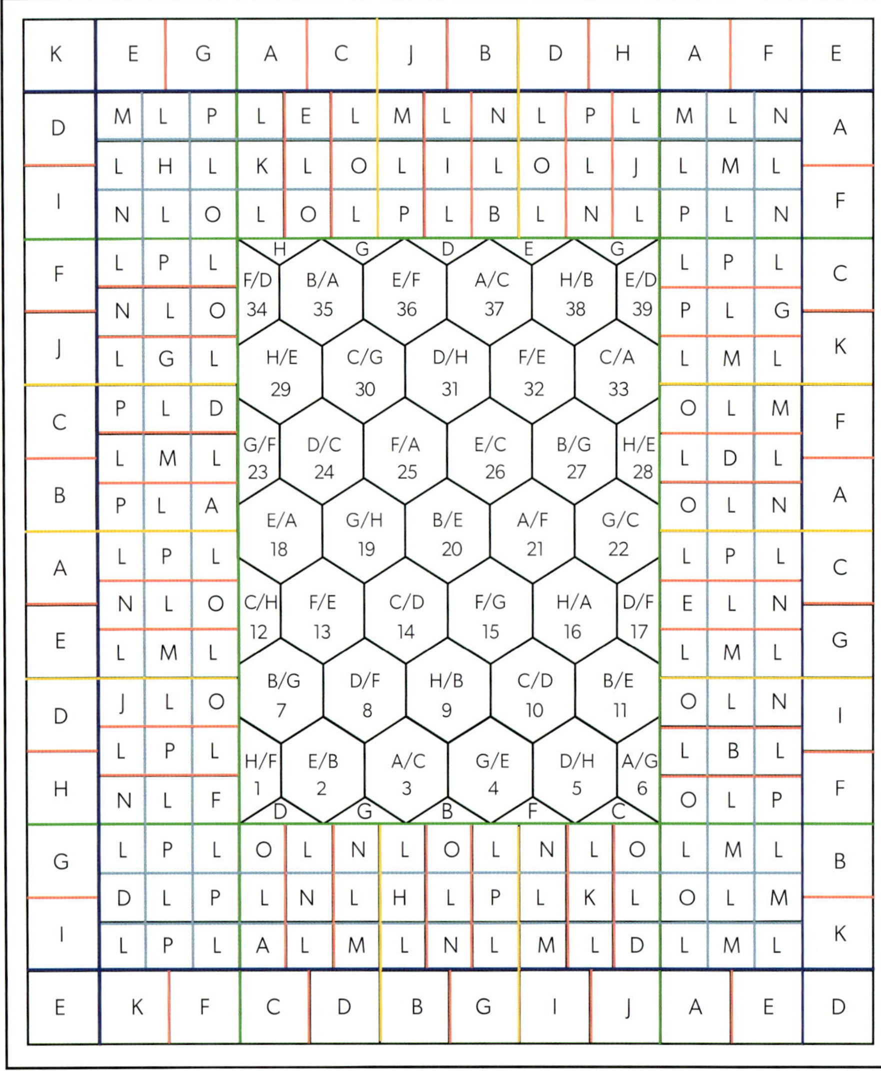

Border Panel – Recommended Seam Joining Order

- First Seams to Join
- Second Seams to Join
- Third Seams to Join
- Fourth Seams to Join
- Fifth Seams to Join

The letters indicate color of yarn used.

The numbers in the center panel indicate order of joining.

Detail of Center Panel Motifs

Center Panel

Two-color hexagon and half-hexagon motifs are worked using colors C1 and C2 as shown in Placement Guide in format "C1/C2". Motif 1 is worked completely without joining, and subsequent motifs are joined as you go using PLT Join on Row/Rnd 6 as instructed (see General Techniques: Joining Methods). Locate number of motif you are working, and follow instructions. For example, if you are on Motif 18, work instructions under the "Motifs 7, 18, and 29" section.

MOTIF 1

Row 1 (RS): With C1, MR, beg dc, [ch1, 2dc] 3 times, ch1, 1dc, turn. [8 dc, 4 ch1-sp]

Row 2: Beg dc in ch-sp, [ch1, 1dc in same sp, 2dc, 1dc in next ch-sp] 3 times, ch1, 1dc in same sp, turn. [14 dc, 4 ch-1sp]

Row 3: Beg dc in ch-sp, [ch1, 1dc in same sp, 4dc, 1dc in next ch-sp] 3 times, ch1, 1dc in same sp, turn. [20 dc, 4 ch-1sp]

Row 4: Beg dc in ch-sp, [ch1, 1dc in same sp, 6dc, 1dc in next ch-sp] 3 times, ch1, 1dc in same sp, turn. [26 dc, 4 ch-1sp]

Row 5: 2sc in first ch-sp, [8sc, 3sc in next ch-sp] 3 times, omitting final sc on third rep, fasten off, do not turn. [34 sc]

Row 6 (RS): With C2, beg dc in first st, 1dc in same st, [10dc, 3dc in next st] 3 times, omitting final dc on third rep, fasten off. [40 dc]

MOTIFS 2–5

Rnd 1 (RS): With C1, MR, beg dc, [ch1, 2dc] 5 times, ch1, 1dc, slst in beg dc. [12 dc, 6 ch1-sp]

Rnd 2: Beg dc in ch-sp, [ch1, 1dc in same sp, 2dc, 1dc in next ch-sp] 6 times, omitting final dc on sixth rep, slst in beg dc. [24 dc, 6 ch1-sp]

Rnd 3: Beg dc in ch-sp, [ch1, 1dc in same sp, 4dc, 1dc in next ch-sp] 6 times, omitting final dc on sixth rep, slst in beg dc. [36 dc, 6 ch1-sp]

Rnd 4: Beg dc in ch-sp, [ch1, 1dc in same sp, 6dc, 1dc in next sp] 6 times, omitting final dc on sixth rep, slst in beg dc. [48 dc, 6 ch-sp]

Rnd 5: [3sc in ch-sp, 8sc] 6 times, slst in first sc, fasten off. [66 sc]

Rnd 6: With C2, beg dc in any cnr sc, 2dc in same st, 10dc, 2dc in next st, PLT in corresponding cnr on adjacent completed motif, 1dc in same st, [PLT, 1dc] 11 times, PLT, 2dc in same st, [10dc, 3dc in next st] 3 times, 10dc, slst in beg dc, fasten off. [78 dc]

MOTIF 6

Rows 1–5: Work as for Motif 1.

Row 6: With C2, beg dc in first st, 1dc in same st, 10dc, 2dc in next st, PLT, 1dc in same st, [PLT, 1dc] 11 times, PLT, 2dc in same st, 10dc, 2dc in final st, fasten off. [40 dc]

MOTIFS 7, 18, AND 29

Rnds 1–5: Work as for Motif 2.

Rnd 6: With C2, beg dc in any cnr sc, 2dc in same st, 10dc, 3dc in next st, 10dc, 2dc in next st, PLT, 1dc in same st, [PLT, 1dc] 11 times across this motif, PLT, 1dc in same st, PLT in cnr dc of next motif, 1dc in same st, [PLT, 1dc] 11 times, 2dc in same st, 10dc, 3dc in next st, 10dc, slst in beg dc, fasten off. [78 dc]

MOTIFS 8–11, 13–16, 19–22, 24–27, 30–33, AND 35–38

Rnds 1–5: Work as for Motif 2.

Rnd 6: With C2, beg dc in any cnr sc, 2dc in same st, 10dc, 2dc in next st, PLT, 1dc in same st, [PLT, 1dc] 11 times across this motif, PLT, 1dc in same st, PLT in cnr dc of next motif, 1dc in same st, [PLT, 1dc] 11 times across next motif, PLT, 1dc in same st, PLT in cnr dc of next motif, 1dc in same st, [PLT, 1dc] 11 times, 2dc in same st, 10dc, 3dc in next st, 10dc, slst in beg dc, fasten off. [78 dc]

MOTIFS 12, 23, AND 34

Rows 1–5: Work as for Motif 1.

Row 6: With C2, beg dc in first st, PLT, 1dc in same st, [PLT, 1dc] 11 times, PLT, 2dc in same st, 10dc, 3dc in next st, 10dc, 2dc in final st, fasten off. [40 dc]

MOTIFS 17, 28, AND 39

Rows 1–5: Work as for Motif 1.

Row 6: With C2, beg dc in first st, 1dc in same st, 10dc, 2dc in next st, PLT, 1dc in same st, [PLT, 1dc] 11 times across this motif, PLT, 1dc in same st, PLT in cnr dc of next motif, 1dc in same st, [PLT, 1dc] 11 times across next motif, PLT, 1dc in same st, fasten off. [40 dc]

FILL TRIANGLE GAPS AT TOP AND BOTTOM EDGES

Row 1: Holding Center Panel with RS facing, join Yarn H in second dc of Motif 35, 1sc in same st, 2sc, 2hdc, 7dc, sk cnr dc of this and next motifs, 7dc, 2hdc, 3sc, turn. [14 dc, 4 hdc, 6 sc]

Row 2 (WS): Slst in first 4 sts, 3sc, 2hdc, 2dc, sk2, 2dc, 2hdc, 3sc, fasten off. [4 dc, 4 hdc, 6 sc]

Fill rem triangle gaps across top edge of blanket in this same manner with colors shown on Placement Guide, then rotate Center Panel to fill 5 triangle gaps across bottom edge of blanket.

Weave in all ends and cont to Center Panel Border.

Center Panel Border Rnd: With Yarn L, slst in first sc of Row 1 on triangle gap at top right cnr of blanket, *3sc in cnr st, 19sc across filled triangle gap, [1sc in cnr dc of hexagon motif, 20sc across filled triangle gap] 4 times, 19sc across final filled triangle gap, 3sc in cnr, [24sc across half-hexagon motif, 14sc across full hexagon motif] 3 times, 25sc across half-hexagon motif; rep from * once more, slst in first sc, fasten off and weave in all ends.

Cont to Border Panel.

Fill Triangle

Border Panel

SMALL SQUARE MOTIF

Make 162 in following color quantities:

Yarn A: 2	Yarn B: 2	Yarn D: 4	Yarn E: 2
Yarn F: 1	Yarn G: 2	Yarn H: 2	Yarn I: 1
Yarn J: 2	Yarn K: 2	Yarn L: 81	Yarn M: 15
Yarn N: 14	Yarn O: 15	Yarn P: 17	

Rnd 1 (RS): MR, beg dc, [ch1, 2dc] 3 times, ch1, 1dc, slst in beg dc. [8 dc, 4 ch-1sp]

Rnd 2: Beg dc in ch-sp, [ch1, 3dc in same sp, 3dc in next ch-sp] 4 times, omitting final dc on fourth rep, slst in beg dc. [24 dc, 4 ch1-sp]

Rnd 3: Beg dc in ch-sp, [ch1, 3dc in same sp, sk3, 3dc between next 2 dc sts, 3dc in next ch-sp] 4 times, omitting final dc on fourth rep, slst in beg dc. [36 dc, 4 ch1-sp]

Rnd 4: [3sc in ch-sp, 9sc] 4 times, slst in first sc, fasten off and weave in ends. [48 sc]

Border Panel

Large Square Motif

LARGE SQUARE MOTIF

Make 48 in following color quantities:

Yarn A: 6	Yarn B: 4	Yarn C: 5	Yarn D: 5
Yarn E: 5	Yarn F: 6	Yarn G: 4	Yarn H: 2
Yarn I: 4	Yarn J: 3	Yarn K: 4	

Rnd 1 (RS): MR, beg 4dc-cl, [ch4, 4dc-cl] 3 times, ch4, slst in beg 4dc-cl. [4 4dc-cl, 4 ch-4sp]

Rnd 2: Beg dc in ch-sp, [7dc in same sp, ch1, 1dc in next ch-sp] 4 times, omitting final dc on fourth rep, slst in beg dc. [32 dc, 4 ch1-sp]

Rnd 3: 1sc in first st, [3sc, ch3, 4sc, 1sc in next ch-sp, 1sc] 4 times, omitting final sc on fourth rep, slst in first sc. [36 sc, 4 ch3-sp]

Rnd 4: Beg dc in first st, *ch1, sk1, 1dc, ch1, (2dc, ch3, 2dc) in next ch-sp, [ch1, sk1, 1dc] 3 times; rep from * 3 times more, omitting final dc on final rep, slst in beg dc. [32 dc, 20 ch1-sp, 4 ch3-sp]

Rnd 5: 1sc in first st, [5sc, 5sc in cnr ch-sp, 8sc] 4 times, omitting final sc on fourth rep, slst in first sc, fasten off and weave in ends. [72 sc]

Join Border Panel Motifs

With Yarn L, join seams in recommended seam joining order as directed in Placement Guide as follows: Attach Yarn L with slst at beg of seam, hold motifs with RS together and Slip-stitch Join (see General Techniques: Joining Methods) across seam to end, working through BLO and holding RS together. Fasten off. Cont to Blanket Border.

Make Blanket Border

Rnd 1: Join Yarn L in top right cnr of blanket, [3sc in cnr st, 17sc across 12 Large Square Motifs, 3sc in cnr st, 17sc across 14 Large Square Motifs] twice, slst in first sc.

Rnd 2: Beg dc in cnr sc, [4dc in same st, 1dc in each st to next cnr sc, 1dc in cnr sc] 4 times, omitting final dc on fourth rep, slst in beg dc.

Rnd 3: 1sc in each st around, slst in first sc, fasten off and weave in ends.

Finishing

Weave in any rem ends and block blanket to given measurements and to flatten seams, being sure to keep rounded corners intact.

HAPPY FLORAL BLANKET

For this project you can use a yarn with long color changes, as I have shown in the sample blanket, or you can choose one or more solid colors for your motifs. However you decide to color your happy flowers, the finished blanket is sure to bring joy to the recipient. Simply add more motifs to the length or width to create the perfectly-sized conversation piece for your room.

Finished Size

45 x 30in (114 x 76cm)

Yarn

Worsted (aran) weight (#4 Medium)

Shown here: Knit Picks Chroma Worsted (70% superwash wool, 30% nylon) 100g (198yd/181m); 1 ball each in following colors:

- Yarn A: Lava Party
- Yarn B: Solar Storm
- Yarn C: Mocktail
- Yarn D: Beatrix
- Yarn E: Ice Lolly
- Yarn F: Clown Wig
- Yarn G: Puffer Jacket

Hook

- US size G/7 (4.5mm) hook

Gauge (Tension)

16 dc x 7 rows = 4 x 4in (10 x 10cm) using a US G/7 (4.5mm) hook.

Pattern Notes

Motifs are worked in order as shown in Placement Guide to make the most of long color changes in yarn.

Motif 1 is completed without joining. All other motifs are joined as you go on final round using PLT Join (see General Techniques: Joining Methods).

Keep all yarn ball leftovers as they will be used in blanket border.

To join new yarns, slst in specified stitch.

Make Blanket Body

Motifs are joined on the final row/rnd in the order number shown in the Placement Guide, from left to right, and bottom to top.

Placement Guide

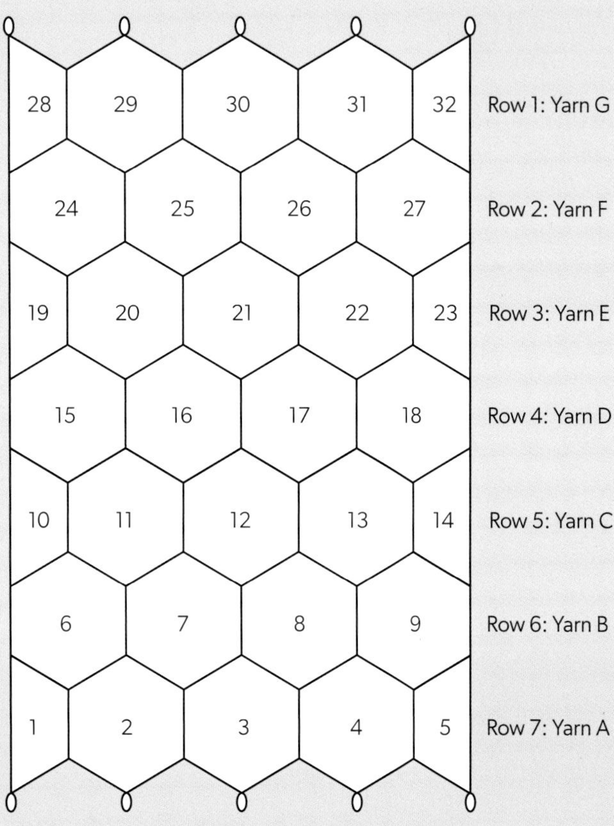

Motif 1

Row 1 (RS): With Yarn A, MR, beg dc, ch1, [2dc-cl, ch2] twice, 2dc-cl, ch1, 1dc, turn. [3 2dc-cl, 2 dc, 4 ch1-sp]

Row 2: Beg dc in first ch-sp, [(pc, ch1, 1dc) in same ch-sp, ch1, 1dc in next ch-sp, ch1] 3 times, (pc, 1dc) in same ch-sp, turn. [4 pc, 8 dc, 9 ch-sp]

Row 3: Beg tr, make Small Petal A as follows: 2tr-cl in next ch-sp stopping before final step (3 lps on hook), 1tr in next dc stopping before final step (4 lps on hook), yoh, draw yarn through all 4 lps – Small Petal A made, [ch6, 1sc in next ch-sp, ch6, make Large Petal as follows: 1tr in next dc stopping before final step (2 lps on hook), [2tr-cl in next ch-sp stopping before final step] twice (6 lps on hook), 1tr in next dc stopping before final step (7 lps on hook), yoh, draw yarn through all 7 lps – Large Petal made] twice, ch6, 1sc in next ch-sp, ch6, make Small Petal B as follows: 1tr in next dc stopping before final step (2 lps on hook), 2tr-cl in next ch-sp stopping before final step (4 lps on hook), yoh, draw yarn through all 4 lps – Small Petal B made, 1tr in final st, turn. [2 Large Petal, 2 Small Petal, 2 tr, 3 sc, 6 ch6-sp]

Row 4: Beg dc, [ch1, 5dc in next ch-sp] 6 times, ch1, 1dc in final st, turn. [32 dc, 7 ch1-sp]

Row 5: 2sc in first ch-sp, [5sc, 1sc in next ch-sp, 5sc, 3sc in next ch-sp] 3 times, omitting final sc on third rep, turn. [43 sc]

Row 6: Beg dc, *ch1, 1dc in same st, [ch1, sk1, 1dc] 7 times; rep from * twice more, ch1, 1dc in same st, fasten off, do not turn. [26 dc, 25 ch1-sp]

Row 7 (RS): Rejoin yarn in first ch-sp, 2sc in same sp, [15sc, 3sc in next ch-sp] 3 times, omitting final sc on third rep, fasten off and weave in ends. [55 sc]

Motifs 2, 3 and 4

Rnd 1: With Yarn A, MR, beg 2dc-cl, [ch2, 2dc-cl] 5 times, ch2, slst in beg 2dc-cl. [6 2dc-cl, 6 ch2-sp]

Rnd 2: Beg dc in first ch-sp, [ch1, (pc, ch1, 1dc) in same ch-sp, ch1, 1dc in next ch-sp] 6 times, omitting final ch1 and 1dc on sixth rep, 1sc in beg dc (counts as final ch1-sp). [6 pc, 12 dc, 18 ch1-sp]

Rnd 3: 1sc in final ch1-sp, *ch6, make Large Petal as in Motif 1, ch6, 1sc in next ch-sp, rep from * 5 times more, omitting final sc on last rep, slst in first sc. [6 large petal, 6 sc, 12 ch-6sp]

Rnd 4: Slst in 2 ch, beg dc in ch-sp, [4dc in same sp, ch1, 1dc in next ch-sp] 12 times, omitting final dc on twelfth rep, slst in beg dc. [60 dc, 12 ch1-sp]

Rnd 5: [1sc in next st, 3sc, 3sc in next ch-sp, 5sc, 1sc in next ch-sp, 1sc] 6 times, slst in first sc. [84 sc]

Rnd 6: Beg dc in next st, *[ch1, sk1, 1dc] twice, ch1, 1dc in same st, [ch1, sk1, 1dc] 5 times, rep from * 5 times more, omitting final dc on last rep, slst in beg dc. [48 dc, 48 ch1-sp]

Rnd 7: 4sc, 3sc in next ch-sp, 15sc, 2sc in next ch-sp, PLT, 1sc in same sp, [PLT, 1sc] 16 times, PLT, 2sc in same sp, [15sc, 3sc in next ch-sp] 3 times, 11sc, slst in first sc, fasten off and weave in ends. [108 sc]

Motif 5

Rows 1–6: With Yarn A, work as for Motif 1, fasten off, do not turn.

Rnd 7 (RS): Rejoin yarn in first ch-sp, 2sc in same sp, 15sc, 2sc in next ch-sp, PLT in cnr sc of Motif 4, 1sc in same sp, [PLT, 1sc] 16 times, PLT, 2sc in same sp, 15sc, 2sc in final ch-sp, fasten off and weave in ends. [55 sc]

Motif 2

Motif 2 Chart

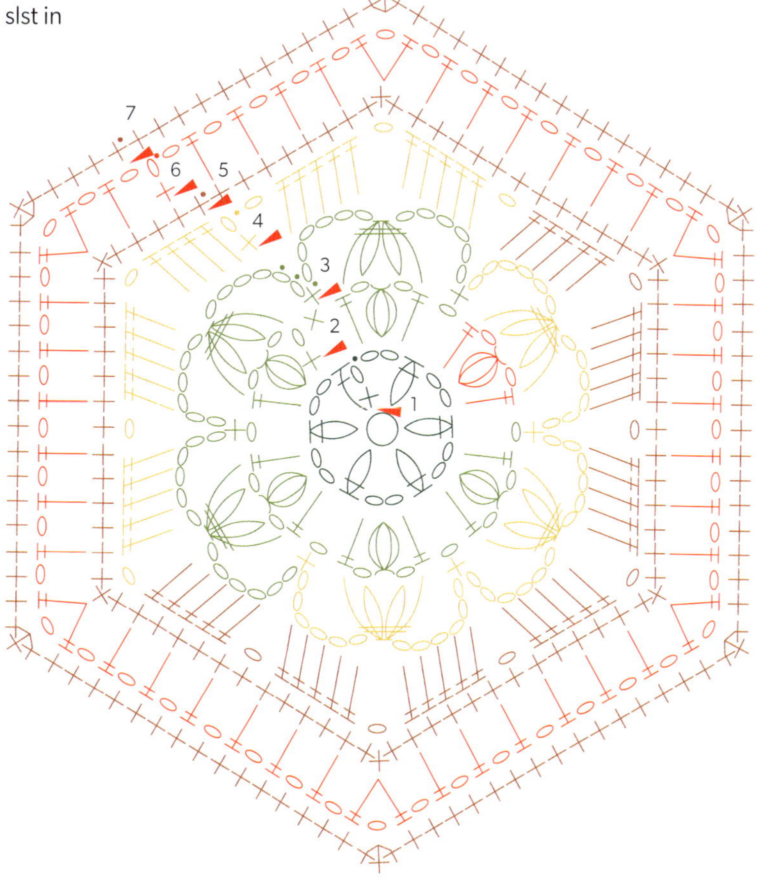

Motifs 6, 15, and 24

Rnds 1–6: With Yarn B, work as for Motif 2.

Rnd 7: 4sc, [3sc in next ch-sp, 15sc] twice, 2sc in next ch-sp, PLT, 1sc in same sp, [PLT, 1sc] 16 times, PLT, 1sc in same sp, PLT in cnr sc of Motif 2, 1sc in same sp, [PLT, 1sc] 16 times, PLT, 2sc in same sp, 15sc, 3sc in next ch-sp, 11sc, slst in first sc, fasten off and weave in ends. [108 sc]

Motifs 7-9, 11-13, 16-18, 20-22, 25-27, and 29-31

Rnds 1–6: With Yarn B, work as for Motif 2.

Rnd 7: 4sc, 3sc in next ch-sp, 15sc, 2sc in next ch-sp, PLT, 1sc in same sp, [PLT, 1sc] 16 times, PLT, 1sc in same sp, PLT in cnr sc of Motif 2, 1sc in same sp, [PLT, 1sc] 16 times, PLT, 1sc in same sp, PLT in cnr sc of Motif 3, 1sc in same sp, [PLT, 1sc] 16 times, PLT, 2sc in same sp, 15sc, 3sc in next ch-sp, 11sc, slst in first sc, fasten off and weave in ends. [108 sc]

Motifs 10, 19, and 28

Rows 1–6: With Yarn C, work as for Motif 1, fasten off, do not turn.

Rnd 7 (RS): Rejoin yarn in first ch-sp, 1sc in same sp, PLT in cnr sc of Motif 6, 1sc in same sp, [PLT, 1sc] 16 times, PLT, 2sc in same sp, [15sc, 3sc in next ch-sp] twice, omitting final sc on second rep, fasten off and weave in ends. [55 sc]

Motifs 14, 23, and 32

Rows 1–6: With Yarn C, work as for Motif 1, fasten off, do not turn.

Rnd 7 (RS): Rejoin yarn in first ch-sp, 2sc in same sp, 15sc, 3sc in next ch-sp, 15sc, 2sc in next ch-sp, PLT in cnr sc of Motif 9, 1sc in same sp, [PLT, 1sc] 16 times, 1sc in same sp, fasten off and weave in ends. [55 sc]

Make Blanket Border

LONG SIDES

With Yarn A until yarn ball is used up, then cont with Yarn B and so on, slst in bottom right cnr of blanket, sc across long side of blanket as follows: [27sc across edge of half-hexagon motifs, 17sc across side of full hexagon motifs] 3 times, 27sc across edge of half-hexagon motifs, fasten off.

Reattach yarn at top left cnr of blanket and rep for opposite long side of blanket, changing to next yarn letter as needed, fasten off.

SHORT SIDES

Short Sides are worked from WS. Tr sts form tiny bobbles on RS of work.

Make faux pompom as follows: [Ch3, 3dc-cl in third ch from hook] twice, slst in same ch as first 3dc-cl to close.

With WS facing, rejoin yarn at bottom left cnr of blanket, 1sc in same st, *ch3, make faux pompom, ch3, 1sc in same st, [1sc in next st, 1tr in next st] 8 times, 1sc, sk cnr sc of next motif, [1sc in next st, 1tr in next st] 8 times, 2sc; rep from * 3 times more, ch3, make faux pompom, ch3, 1sc in same st, fasten off.

Reattach yarn on opposing short side and rep, fasten off and weave in ends.

Finishing

Weave in any rem ends and block blanket to given measurements and to open up floral design.

FRUIT PIE BLANKET

I drew inspiration from a colorful abstract wall mural for this blanket – but when the design was finished it made me think of a fruit pie with a lattice crust, and so the Fruit Pie Blanket was born. With bold blocks of color featured on diagonal geometric panels, every joined block is exciting! Choose any four colors and bake up a masterpiece.

Finished Size

48 x 36in (122 x 91.5cm)

Yarn

Light worsted (DK) weight (#3 Light)

Shown here: Scheepjes Scrumptious (50% recycled polyester (recycled plastic bottles), 50% acrylic) 100g (328yd/300m); 1 ball each in following colors, unless otherwise specified:

- Yarn A: 311 Chai Shortbread; 2 balls
- Yarn B: 308 Grapefruit Curd Tart
- Yarn C: 332 Orange Cheesecake
- Yarn D: 343 French Blue Macaron

Hook

- US size G/6 (4mm) hook

Gauge (Tension)

16 dc x 9 rows = 4 x 4in (10 x 10cm) using a US G/6 (4mm) hook.

Pattern Notes

Sections are worked separately and then joined with Whip-stitch Join (see General Techniques: Joining Methods).

Weave in ends as you go for easier finish.

To join new yarns, slst in specified stitch.

Make Blanket Body

Section 1

Row 1 (RS): With Yarn C, MR, beg dc, 4dc, turn. [5 dc]

Row 2: (Beg dc, 2dc) in first st, 1dc in each st to final st, 3dc in final st, turn. [4 sts inc]

Row 3: (Beg dc, 1dc) in first st, 1dc in each st to final st, 2dc in final st, turn. [2 sts inc]

Rows 4 and 5: Rep Row 2 twice more. [19 dc]

Fasten off, do not turn.

Join Yarn D to first st, ready to work another RS row.

Row 6 (RS): Rep Row 3. [21 dc]

Rows 7 and 8: Rep Row 2 twice more. [29 dc]

Row 9: Rep Row 3. [31 dc]

Row 10: Rep Row 2, fasten off, do not turn. [35 dc]

Join Yarn C to first st, ready to work another RS row.

Rows 11–14: Rep Rows 2 and 3 twice more, turn. [47 dc]

Section 1 Border Rnd (RS): 3sc in first st, 50sc evenly across side, 3sc in next st, 36sc evenly across side, 3sc in cnr, 36sc evenly across side, slst in first sc, fasten off and weave in ends. [131 dc]

Section 2

Work as for Section 1, with Yarn A on Rows 1–5, 11–15, and on Border Rnd, and Yarn C on Rows 6–10.

Section 3

Motifs are worked separately and joined with Whipstitch Join (see General Techniques: Joining Methods) according to layout in Placement Guide.

MOTIF 1 (MAKE 3)

Rnd 1 (RS): With Yarn B, MR, beg dc, 15dc, slst in beg dc. [16 dc]

Rnd 2: (Beg dc, 1dc) in first st, 2dc in each of next 15 sts, slst in beg dc. [32 dc]

Section 2 Striped Corner

Section 3 Motif 1

Rnd 3: (Beg dc, 1dc) in first st, [1dc, 2dc in next st] 15 times, 1dc, slst in beg dc, fasten off. [48 dc]

With RS facing, join Yarn A in any st.

Rnd 4: Beg tr in same st, [ch2, 2tr in same st, 2dc, 1hdc, 5sc, 1hdc, 2dc, 2tr in next st] 4 times, omitting final tr on fourth rep, slst in beg tr. [16 tr, 16 dc, 8 hdc, 20 sc, 4 ch2-sp]

Rnd 5: [3sc in ch2-sp, 15sc] 4 times, slst in first sc, fasten off and weave in ends. [72 sc]

MOTIF 2 (MAKE 6)

Row 1 (RS): With Yarn B, MR, beg dc, 8dc, turn. [9 dc]

Row 2: Beg dc, 2dc in each of next 8 sts, turn. [17 dc]

Row 3: Beg dc, [2dc in next st, 1dc] 8 times, fasten off, do not turn. [25 dc]

Join Yarn A in first st, ready to work another RS row.

Row 4 (RS): (Beg tr, ch1, 2tr) in first st, 2dc, 1hdc, 5sc, 1hdc, 2dc, (2tr, ch2, 2tr) in next st, 2dc, 1hdc, 5sc, 1hdc, 2dc, (2tr, ch1, 1tr) in final st, fasten off, do not turn. [10 tr, 8 dc, 4 hdc, 10 sc, 2 ch1-sp, 1 ch2-sp]

Join Yarn A in first ch-sp, ready to work another RS row.

Row 5 (RS): 2sc in first ch-sp, 15sc, 3sc in next ch-sp, 15sc, 2sc in final ch-sp, fasten off and weave in ends. [37 sc]

Section 3 Motif 2

JOIN MOTIFS

Lay Motifs 1 and 2 out as shown in Placement Guide. With Yarn A, seam motifs together with Whip-stitch Join (see General Techniques: Joining Methods). Cont to Section 3 Border Rnd.

Section 3 Border Rnd (RS): Join Yarn A in uppermost cnr, 3sc in cnr, 25sc evenly across each of 4 Motif 2, 3sc in cnr, 18sc across Motif 2, 18sc across Motif 1, 3sc in cnr, 25sc evenly across each of next 2 Motif 2, 3sc in cnr, 18sc across Motif 1, 18sc across Motif 2, slst in first sc, fasten off and weave in ends. [234 sc]

Section 4

MOTIF 1 (MAKE 2)

With Yarns D and B, work as for Motif 1 in Section 3.

MOTIF 2 (MAKE 6)

With Yarns D and B, work as for Motif 2 in Section 3.

Join motifs with reference to Section 4 in Placement Guide. Cont to Section 4 Border Rnd.

Section 4 Border Rnd (RS): Join Yarn A in uppermost cnr, 3sc in cnr, 18sc across Motif 2, 18sc across Motif 1, 3sc in cnr, 25sc evenly across each of next 2 Motif 2, 3sc in cnr, 23sc evenly across Motif 2, 3sc in cnr, 25sc evenly across each of next 3 Motif 2, slst in first sc, fasten off and weave in ends. [196 sc]

Section 5

Row 1 (RS): With Yarn C, ch77, 1dc in third ch from hook (turning ch counts as 1 dc), 72dc, 3dc in next ch, turn. [77 dc]

Row 2: (Beg dc, 2dc) in first st, 1dc in each st to end, turn. [2 sts inc]

Placement guide

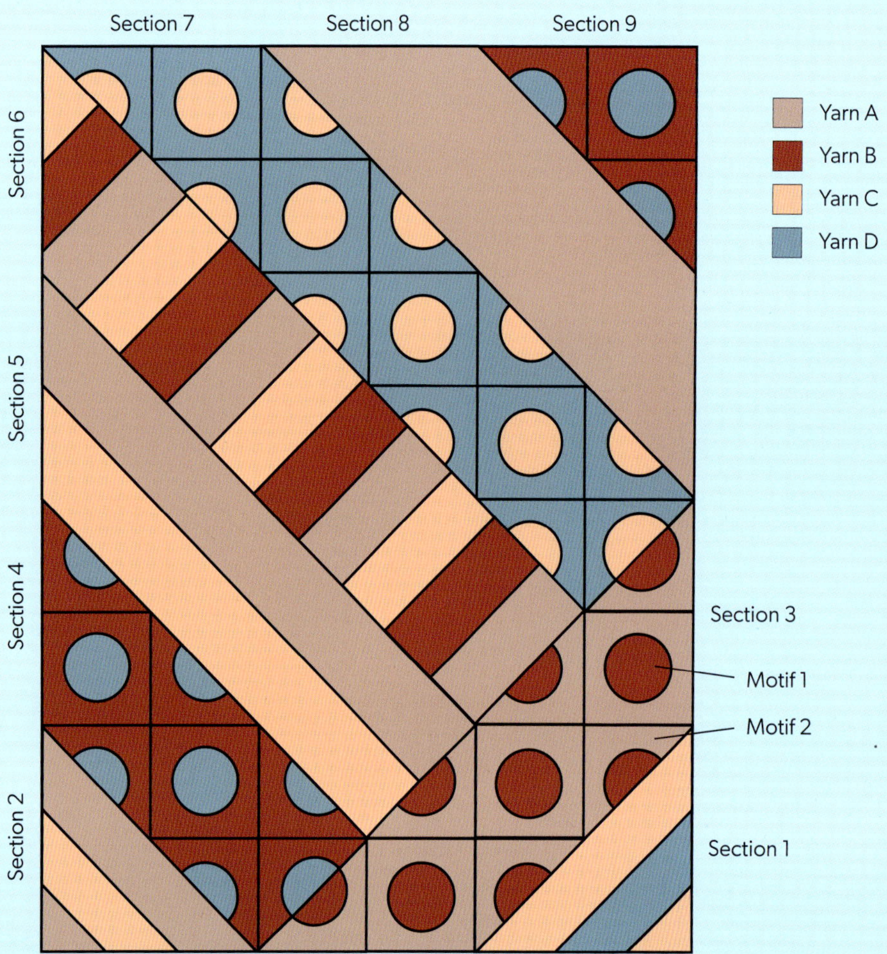

Row 3: Beg dc, 1dc in each st to final st, 2dc in final st, turn. [1 st inc]

Row 4: Rep Row 2. [2 sts inc]

Row 5: Beg dc, 1dc in each st to final st, 3dc in final st, turn. [2 sts inc]

Row 6: (Beg dc, 1dc) in first st, 1dc in each st to end, fasten off, turn. [1 st inc]

Row 7 (RS): Join Yarn A in first st, work as for Row 5. [87 dc]

Rows 8–12: Rep Rows 2–6. [95 dc]

Fasten off and weave in ends.

Section 5 Border Rnd: With RS facing, join Yarn A in uppermost cnr, 3sc in cnr, 36sc evenly across side, 3sc in cnr, 75sc across starting chs, 3sc in cnr, 21sc evenly across side, 3sc in cnr, 93sc, slst in first sc, fasten off and weave in ends. [237 sc]

Section 6

Row 1 (RS): With Yarn A, ch25, 1dc in third ch from hook (turning ch counts as 1 dc), 21dc, turn. [23 dc]

Rows 2–4: Beg dc, 22dc, turn.

Row 5: Beg dc, 22dc, fasten off, do not turn.

Join Yarn B to first st, ready to work another RS row.

Row 6 (RS): Beg dc in first st, 22dc, turn.

Rows 7–10: Rep Rows 2–5.

Rows 11–15: Rep Rows 6–10, using Yarn C.

Rows 16–20: Rep Rows 6–10, using Yarn A.

Rows 21–40: Rep Rows 6–20, then Rows 6–10.

Rows 41–45: Rep Rows 11–15.

Join Yarn A in first st, ready to work another RS row.

Rows 46–49: Beg dc, 22dc, turn.

Row 50 (RS): Beg dc, 19dc, dc3tog, fasten off, do not turn. [21 sts]

Join Yarn B in first st, ready to work another RS row.

Row 51 (RS): Beg dc, 17dc, dc3tog, turn. [19 sts]

Row 52: Beg dc2tog, 17dc, turn. [18 sts]

Row 53: Beg dc, 14dc, dc3tog, turn. [16 sts]

Row 54: Beg dc3tog, 13dc, turn. [14 sts]

Row 55: Beg dc, 11dc, dc2tog, fasten off, do not turn. [13 sts]

Join Yarn C to first st, ready to work another RS row.

Row 56 (RS): Beg dc, 9dc, dc3tog, turn. [11 sts]

Row 57: Beg dc3tog, 8dc, turn. [9 sts]

Row 58: Beg dc, 6dc, dc2tog, turn. [8 sts]

Row 59: Beg dc3tog, 5dc, turn. [6 sts]

Row 60: Beg dc, 2dc, dc3tog, turn. [4 sts]

Row 61: Beg dc4tog, fasten off and weave in ends.

Section 6 Border Rnd: With RS facing, join Yarn A to uppermost cnr, 3sc in cnr, 36sc evenly across side, 3sc in cnr, 75sc evenly across side, working in side of each dc, 3sc in cnr, 21sc evenly across side, 3sc in cnr, 125sc evenly across side, slst in first sc, fasten off and weave in ends. [269 sc]

Section 6

Section 7

MOTIF 1 (MAKE 4)

With Yarns C and D, work as for Motif 1 in Section 3.

MOTIF 2 (MAKE 10)

With Yarns C and D, work as for Motif 2 in Section 3.

Join motifs as before, laying out motifs as shown for Section 7 in Placement Guide. Cont to Section 7 Border Rnd.

Section 7 Border Rnd: Join Yarn A in top left cnr, 3sc in cnr, 25sc evenly across each of 5 Motif 2, 3sc in cnr, 21sc evenly across Motif 2, 3sc in cnr, 25sc evenly across each of next 4 Motif 2, 3sc in cnr, 18sc across Motif 1, 18sc across Motif 2, slst in first sc, fasten off and weave in ends. [294 sc]

Section 8

Row 1 (RS): With Yarn A, MR, beg dc, 2dc, turn. [3 dc]

Row 2: (Beg dc, 2dc) in first st, 1dc in each st to end, turn. [2 sts inc]

Row 3: Beg dc, 1dc in each sts to final st, 2dc in final st, turn. [1 st inc]

Row 4: Rep Row 2. [8 dc]

Row 5: Beg dc, 1dc in each st to final st, 3dc in final st, turn. [2 sts inc]

Row 6: (Beg dc, 1dc) in first st, 1dc in each st to end, turn. [1 st inc]

Row 7: Rep Row 5. [13 dc]

Rows 8 and 9: Rep Rows 2 and 3. [16 dc]

Rows 10–13: Rep Rows 2, 5, 3 and 5. [18 dc]

Rows 14–38: Beg dc, 22dc, turn.

Row 39: Beg dc, 1dc in each st to last 3 sts, dc3tog. [2 sts dec]

Row 40: Beg dc3tog, 1dc in each st to end, turn. [2 sts dec]

Row 41: Beg dc, 1dc in each st until 2 sts rem, dc2tog. [1 st dec]

Row 42: Rep Row 40. [2 sts dec]

Row 43: Rep Row 39. [2 sts dec]

Row 44: Beg dc2tog, 1dc in each st to end, turn. [1 st dec]

Rows 45–50: Rep Rows 39–44. [3 sts]

Row 51: Beg dc3tog, do not fasten off, do not turn.

Section 8 Border Rnd (RS): 3sc in cnr, 36sc evenly across side, 3sc in cnr, 50sc evenly across side, 3sc in cnr, 36sc evenly across side, 3sc in cnr, 100sc evenly across side, slst in first sc, fasten off and weave in ends. [234 sc]

Section 9

MOTIF 1 (MAKE 1)

With Yarns D and B, work as for Motif 1 in Section 3.

MOTIF 2 (MAKE 2)

With Yarns D and B, work as for Motif 2 in Section 3.

Join motifs according to Section 9 in Placement Guide. Cont to Section 9 Border Rnd.

Section 9 Border Rnd: Join Yarn A in top left cnr, 3sc in cnr st, 25sc evenly across next 2 Motif 2, 3sc in cnr, 18sc evenly across Motif 2, 18sc evenly across Motif 1, 3sc in cnr, 18sc evenly across Motif 1, 18sc evenly across Motif 2, slst in first sc, fasten off and weave in ends. [131 sc]

Join Sections

With Yarn A, join seams with Whip-stitch Join (see General Techniques: Joining Methods). Cont to Blanket Border.

Make Blanket Border

Rnd 1: Join Yarn A in top right cnr of blanket, [3sc in cnr, 38sc evenly across next 3 sections, 3sc in cnr, 38sc evenly across next 4 sections] twice, slst in first sc, fasten off and weave in ends. [544 sc]

Finishing

Weave in any rem ends and block blanket to given measurements and to flatten seams.

GENERAL TECHNIQUES

Make Ring (MR)

Ch3, insert the hook in the first chain (not into the slip knot), yarn over hook and pull through both the chain and the loop on the hook (A) to complete the chain ring (B).

Slip Stitch (slst)

Insert the hook into the stitch from front to back, yarn over (C). Pull the yarn through the stitch and through the loop on the hook (D).

Single Crochet (sc)

Insert the hook into the top of the first stitch from front to back (E), yarn over and pull through the stitch (two loops on the hook). Yarn over again and pull through both loops on the hook (F) to finish the stitch (G).

Half Double Crochet (hdc)

Yarn over, insert the hook into the top of the stitch from front to back (H), yarn over and pull the yarn through the stitch (three loops on the hook) (I). Yarn over and pull through all three loops on the hook to finish the stitch (J).

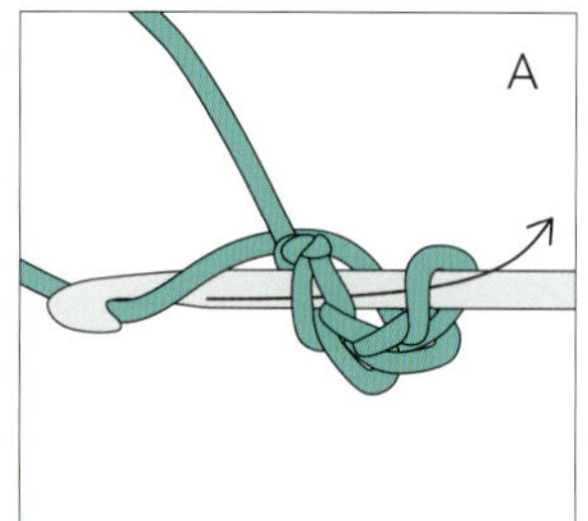

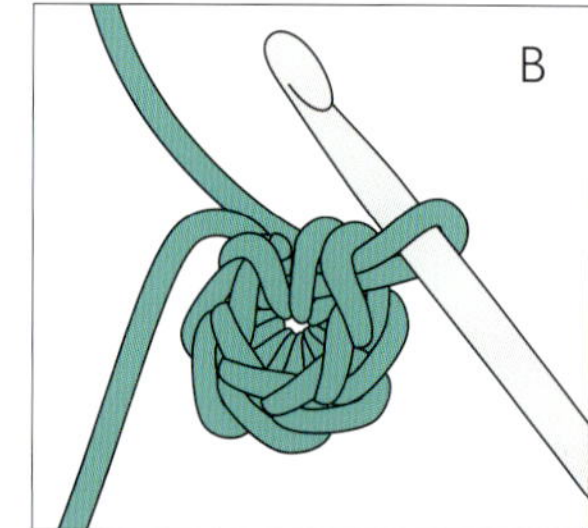

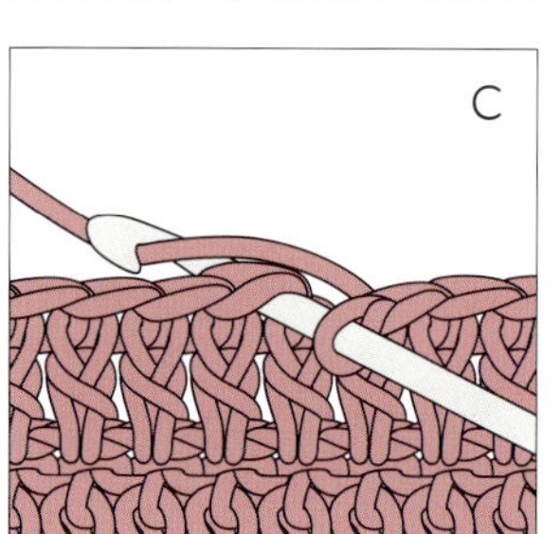

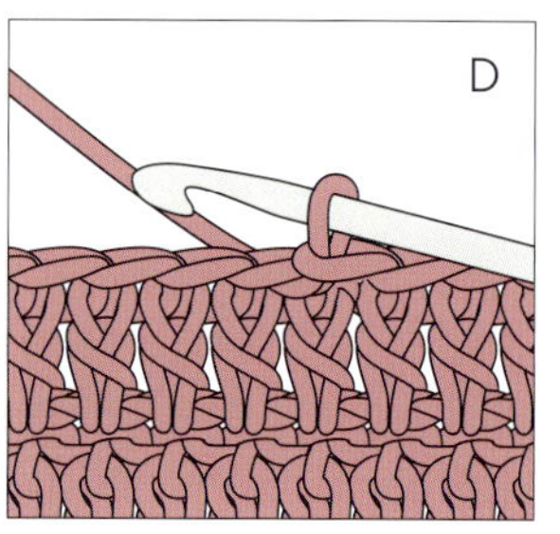

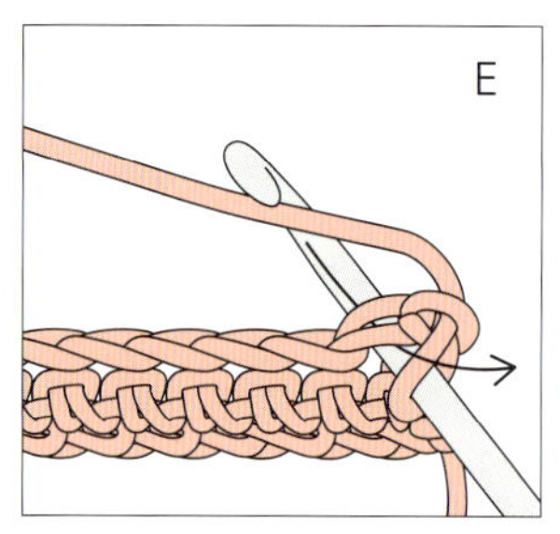

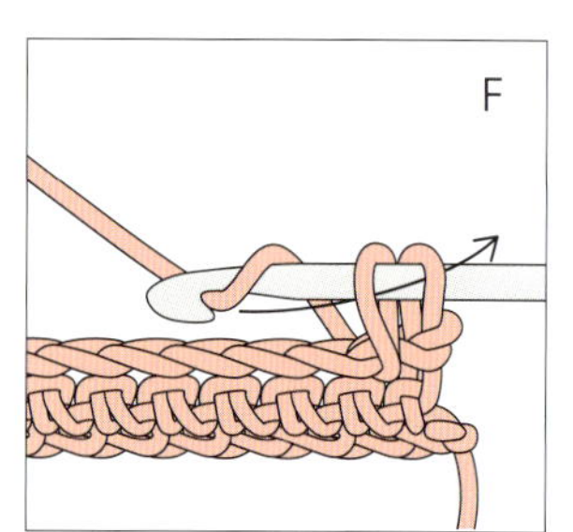

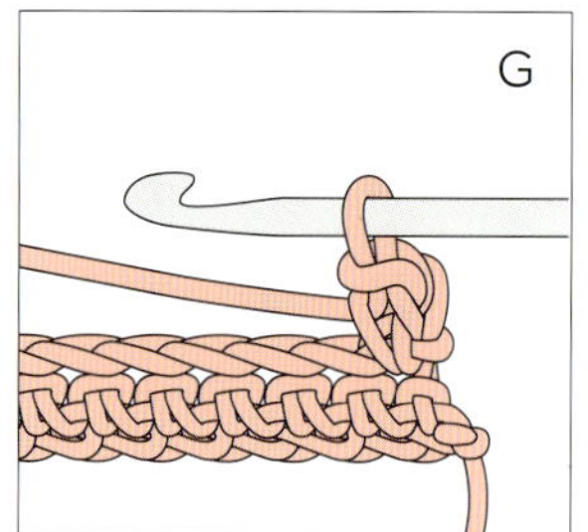

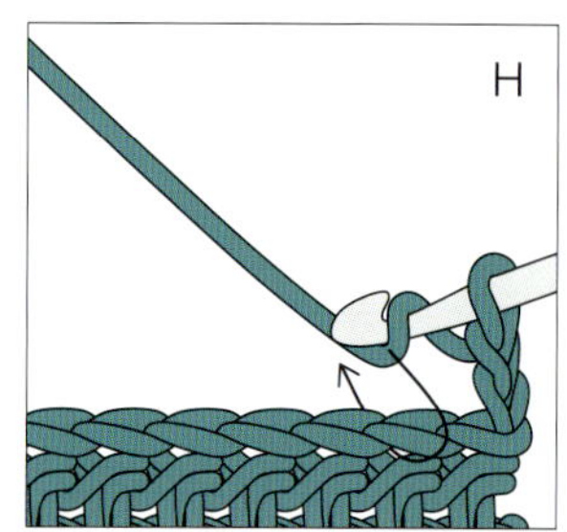

Double Crochet (dc)

Yarn over, insert the hook into the top of the stitch from front to back (K). Yarn over and pull through the stitch (three loops on the hook), yarn over, pull through the first two loops on the hook (two loops on the hook), yarn over and pull through the remaining two loops on the hook to finish the stitch (L).

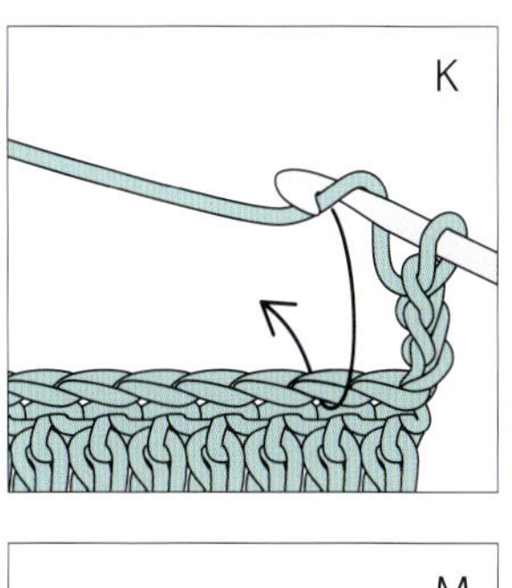

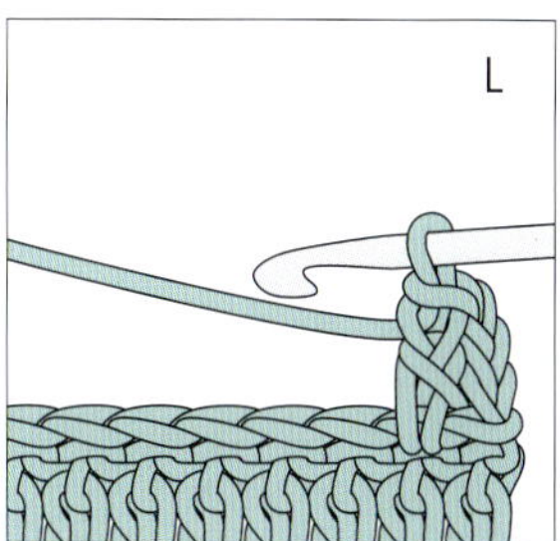

Treble Crochet (tr)

Yarn over twice, insert the hook into the top of the stitch from front to back (M). Yarn over and pull through the stitch (four loops on the hook). Yarn over, pull through the first two loops on the hook (three loops on the hook). Yarn over and pull through next two loops on the hook (N) (two loops on the hook), yarn over and pull through the last two loops to finish the stitch.

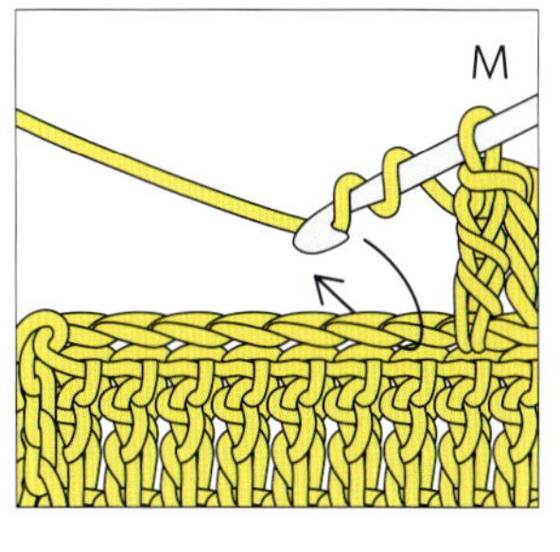

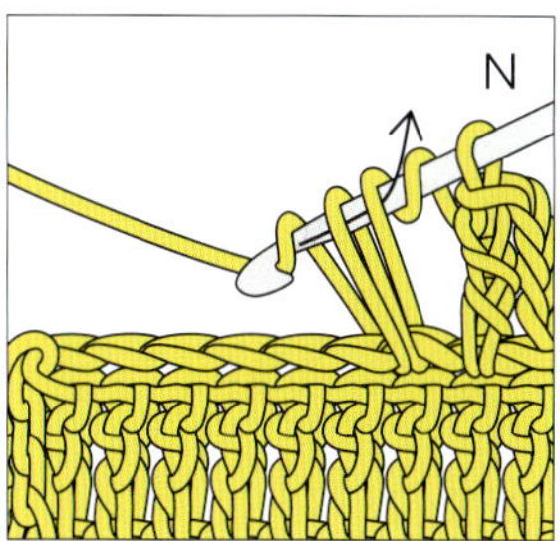

Back Post/Front Post (BP/FP)

Instead of working into the top of the stitch, you'll work around the 'post' of the stitch below. These illustrations show a Front and Back Post Double crochet (FPdc and BPdc) being worked. For Front Post crochet, insert the hook from the back, around the front of the stitch, through to the back again (O). For Back Post crochet, insert the hook from the front, around the back of the stitch, through to the front again (P).

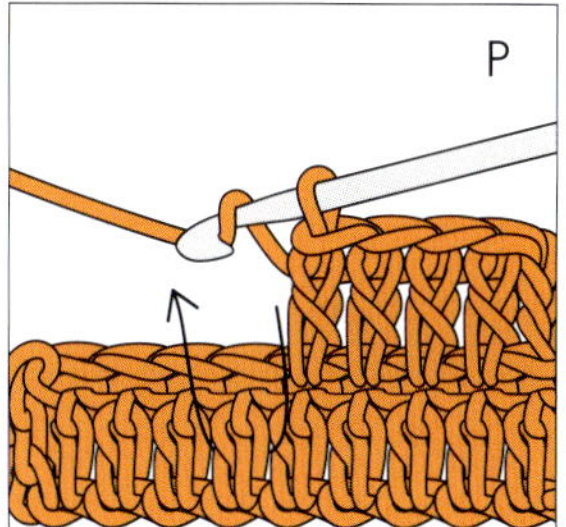

Back Loop Only /Front Loop Only (BLO/FLO)

Some stitches require that you work only into the back (Q) or front (R) loop on the top of the stitch.

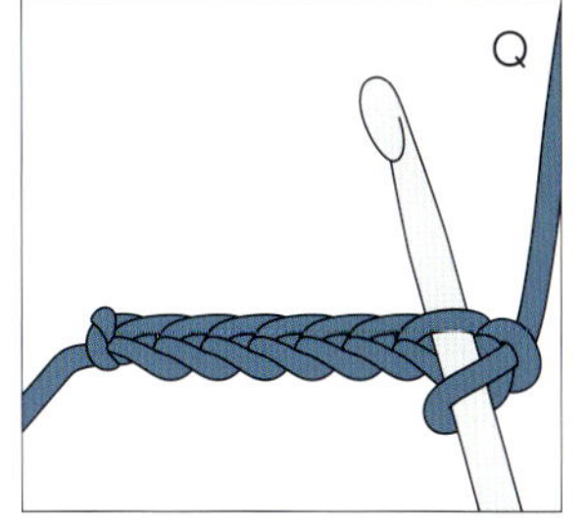

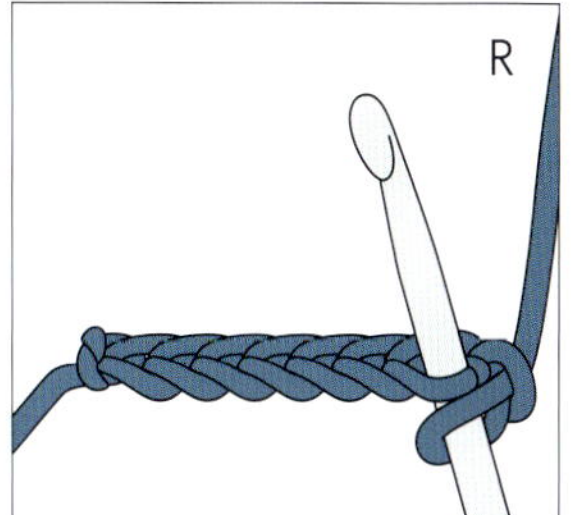

Weaving in Ends

Use a tapestry needle to weave your ends into the wrong side of the work each time you cut the yarn. This means you have less weaving in to do at the end!

Joining Methods

Slip-stitch Join

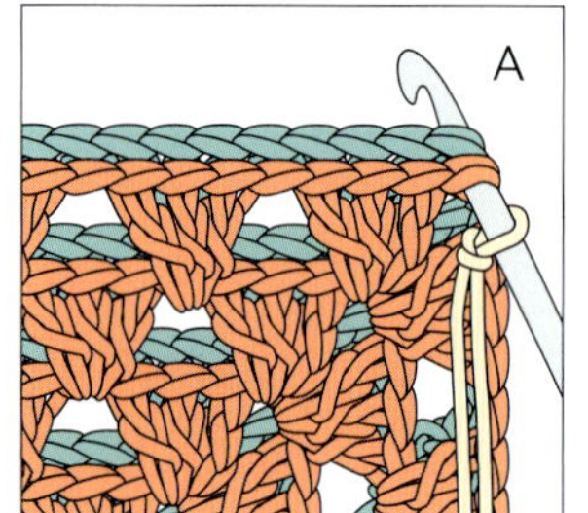

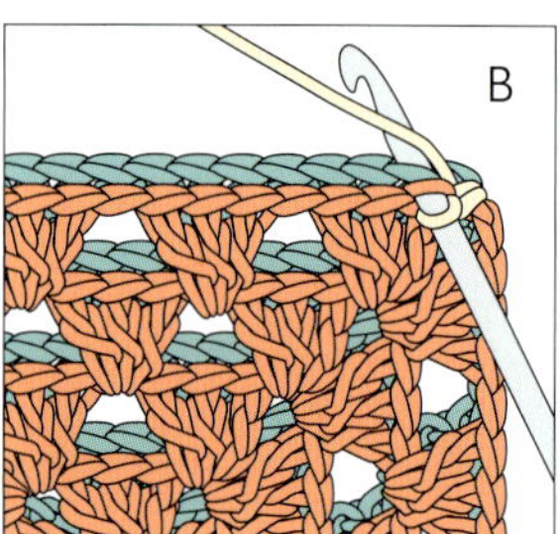

This is worked through back loops only (BLO) or through both loops of each motif depending on the pattern. Begin with a slip knot on the hook. Holding the motifs with either right sides or wrong sides together as instructed, insert the hook in both loops of the first stitch of both pieces (A) and work a slip stitch to join the yarn. Here the motifs are right sides together. Insert the hook into the BLO of the next stitch on both pieces, yarn over (B) and work a slip stitch. Continue in this way working across the seam to the end. Fasten off.

Whip-stitch Join

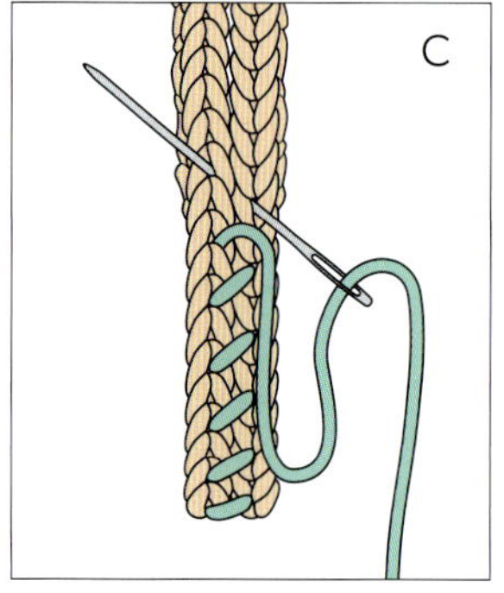

Hold two motifs with wrong sides together, and use your hook to pull the long tail of one of the motifs through the center sc of both motifs, from back to front.

Insert the hook front to back through both loops of the next st to the left, on both motifs. Grab the long tail and pull it all the way through to the front of the piece, allowing the whip stitch to rest flush against the top edge of the motifs (C). Repeat across the seam, inserting the hook through both motifs from front to back in the next st to the left, and pulling the yarn through to the front.

When the next corner is reached, if there are no more sides to join, you can weave in the excess tail, trimming it if necessary.

If there are more sides to join, do so, then cut yarn shorter if needed and weave in ends. Do not pull yarn tail to tighten whip stitches, as it will pull the yarn through the whole join, causing it to bunch.

Pull-loop-through Join (PLT Join)

The PLT is a simple technique for connecting motifs. Use this method to join motifs as you go as follows:

Remove the loop from your hook. Insert the hook from front to back through the corresponding st/sp of the adjoining motif. Return the loop to the hook (D) and pull it to the front of the work (E). Work the stitch as instructed – the stitch shown is a dc (F). Repeat steps 1–5 to end (G).

When joining hexagons, work the join in the order shown in the diagram.

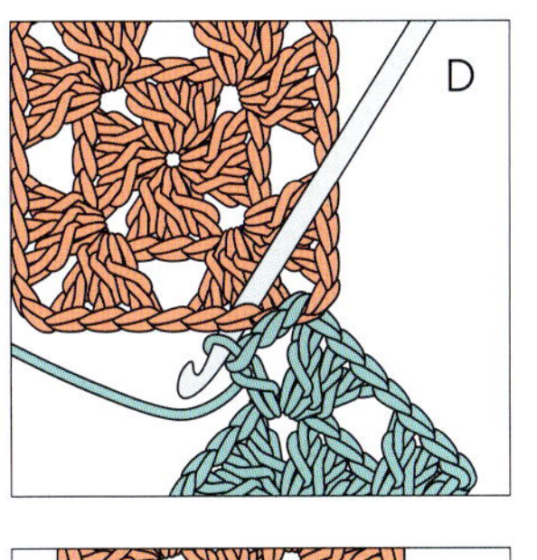

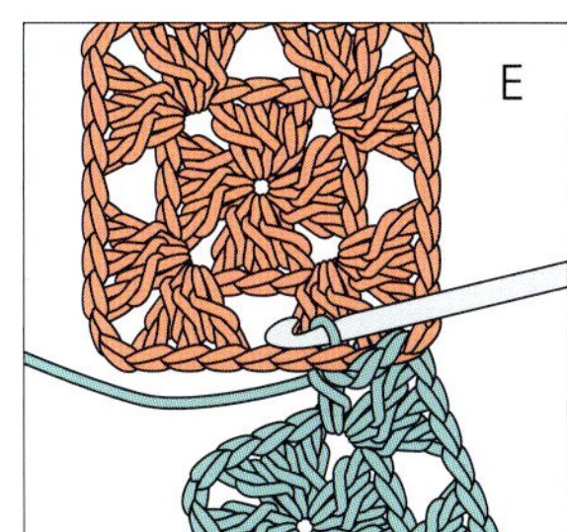

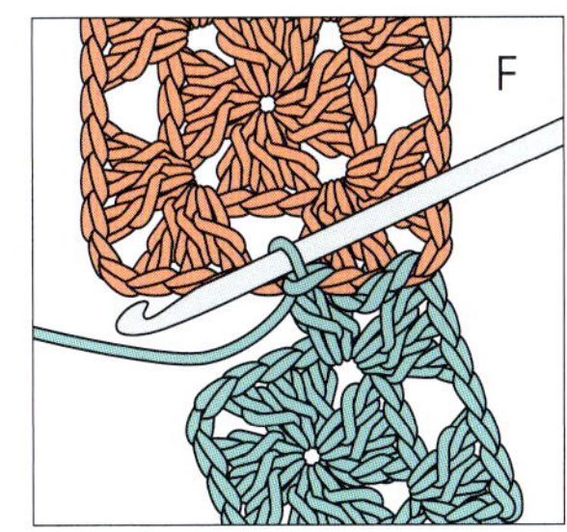

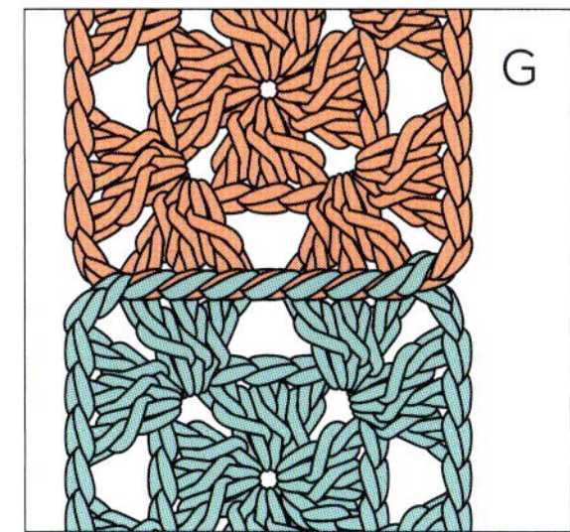

Joining hexagons with a PLT join

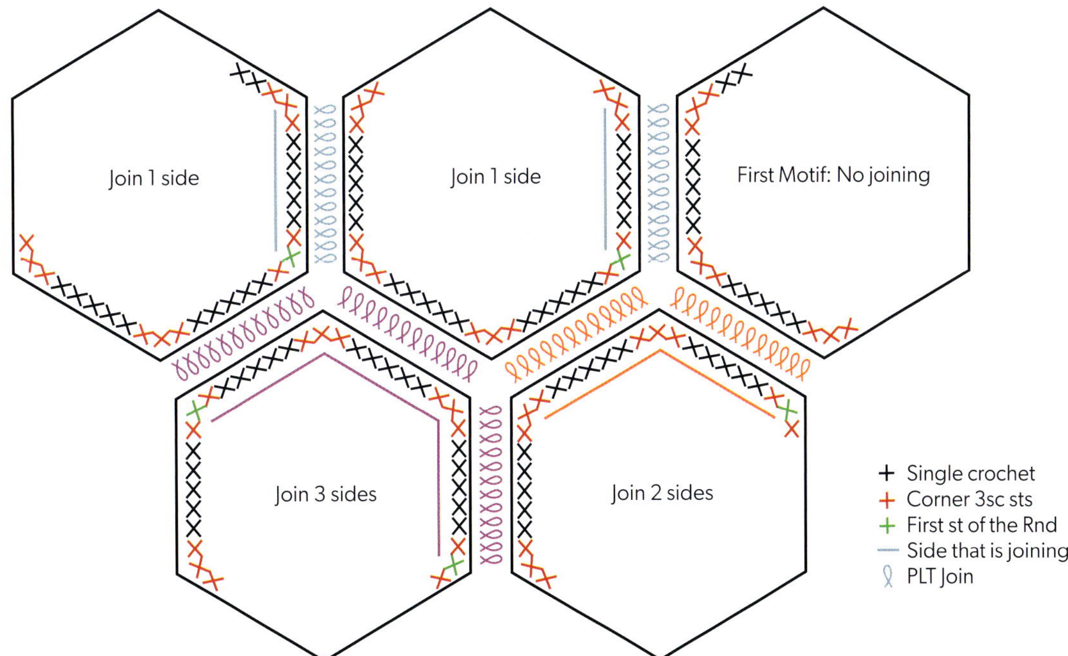

STITCH GUIDE

Conversion Table

US crochet terminology is used throughout this book. The UK equivalents are given here.

US	UK
single crochet (sc)	double crochet (dc)
half double (hdc)	half treble (htr)
double crochet (dc)	treble (tr)
treble (tr)	double treble (dtr)

Abbreviations

2dc-cl (2dc cluster): [yoh, insert hook in st/sp, yoh, pull up lp, yoh, draw yarn through 2 lps] twice, yoh, draw yarn through all 3 lps

2tr-cl (2tr cluster): *yoh twice, insert hook in st/sp, yoh, pull up lp, [yoh, draw yarn through 2 lps] twice; rep from * once, yoh, draw yarn through all 3 lps

3dc-cl (3dc cluster): [yoh, insert hook in st/sp, yoh, pull up lp, yoh, draw yarn through 2 lps] 3 times, yoh, draw yarn through all 4 lps

3tr-cl (3tr cluster): *yoh twice, insert hook in st, yoh, pull through, [yoh, pull through 2 lps] twice; rep from * twice, yoh and pull through all 4 lps

4dc-cl (4dc cluster): [yoh, insert hook in st/sp, yoh, pull up lp, yoh, draw yarn through 2 lps] 4 times, yoh, draw yarn through all 5 lps

4tr-cl (4tr cluster): *yoh twice, insert hook in st, yoh, pull through, [yoh, pull through 2 lps] twice; rep from * 3 times more, yoh and pull through all 5 lps

beg: beginning

beg 2dc-cl: (beg dc, dc) in st/sp indicated; when joining rnd, slst in full dc st

beg 2tr-cl: (beg tr, 1tr) in st/sp; counts as 1 2tr-cl

beg 3dc-cl: (beg dc, 2dc-cl) in same st/sp; counts as 1 3dc-cl

beg 3tr-cl: beg tr, *yoh twice, insert hook in st, yoh, pull through, [yoh, pull through 2 lps] twice; rep from * once more, yoh and pull through all 3 lps

beg 4dc-cl: (beg dc, 3dc-cl) in same st/sp; counts as 1 4dc-cl

beg 4tr-cl: beg tr, *yoh twice, insert hook in same st, yoh, pull through, [yoh, pull through 2 lps] twice, rep from * twice more, yoh and pull through all 4 lps

beg dc: (sc, ch1); counts as 1 dc

beg dc2tog: beg dc, 1dc in next st; when joining rnd, slst in full dc

beg dc3tog: beg dc, [yoh, insert hook in next st/sp, yoh, pull through, yoh, pull through 2 lps] twice, yoh, pull through all 3 lps; when joining rnd, slst in full decrease

beg dc4tog: beg dc, [yoh, insert hook in next st/sp, yoh, pull through, yoh, pull through 2 lps] 3 times, yoh, pull through all 4 lps; when joining rnd, slst in full decrease

beg dc5tog: beg dc, [yoh, insert hook in next st/sp, yoh, pull through, yoh, pull through 2 lps] 4 times, yoh, pull through all 5 lps; when joining rnd, slst in full decrease

beg hdc: (sc, ch1); counts as 1 hdc

beg pc (beginning popcorn): (beg dc, 3dc) in st/sp, release lp from hook, insert hook from front to back through beg dc, grab lp and pull through to front of work to close popcorn

beg tr: (1sc, ch2); counts as 1 tr

BLO: work in back lps only (see General Techniques)

bobble: [yoh, insert hook in st/sp, yoh, pull up lp, yoh, pull yarn through 2 lps] 4 times, yoh, pull yarn through 5 lps

BP: back post (see General Techniques)

chX: chain X number of times (see General Techniques)

cnr: corner

cont: continu(e)ing

dec: decreas(ed)ing

dc: double crochet (see General Techniques)

dc2tog: [yoh insert hook in next st/sp, yoh, pull through, yoh, pull through 2 lps] twice, yoh, pull through all 3 lps

dc3tog: [yoh, insert hook in next st/sp, yoh, pull through yoh, pull through 2 lps] 3 times, yoh, pull through all 4 lps

dc4tog: [yoh, insert hook in next st/sp, yoh, pull through, yoh, pull through 2 lps] 4 times, yoh, pull through all 5 lps

dc5tog: [yoh, insert hook in next st/sp, yoh, pull through, yoh, pull through 2 lps] 5 times, yoh, pull through all 6 lps

FLO: work in front lps only (see General Techniques)

FP: front post (see General Techniques)

hdc: half double crochet (see General Techniques)

inc: increas(ed)ing

lp: loop

MR: make ring (see General Techniques)

pc (popcorn): 4dc in st/sp, release lp from hook, insert hook from front to back through first dc, grab lp, pull through to front of work to close popcorn

picot: ch3, 1sc in third ch from hook to close picot

PLT (pull lp through): See Joining Methods

PM: place marker

rem: remaining

rep: repeat

RS: right side

sc: single crochet (see General Techniques)

sk: skip

sp: space (ch-sp = chain space)

slst: slip stitch (see General Techniques)

st(s): stitch(es)

tog: together

tr: treble crochet (see General Techniques)

WS: wrong side

yoh: yarn over hook

ABOUT THE AUTHOR

Rachele Carmona is the crochet/knit pattern designer behind Cypress Textiles. She holds a Bachelor of Arts degree in English Rhetoric from Texas A&M University. Her needle-crafts career began as a college hobby, which grew to new heights after encouragement from her close friends and the creative community. Eventually, she left her job as a restaurant manager to stay home with her budding family and focus on her craft. Rachele resides in the Houston area with her husband, and their four children and four fur-babies.

ACKNOWLEDGMENTS

Creating these designs and crafting them into a book has been equal parts challenging and rewarding, just as a great life experience should be. I would like to thank Sarah Callard who approached me to write this book, and everyone on the David and Charles team. Special thanks to Rachael Prest, Jess Pearson, Marie Clayton, and the other editors who gave their blessings and encouragement.

The bulk of my gratitude on this journey goes to my family. So many thanks to my extraordinary husband, Nicolas, and our four children, who provide never-ending love, confidence, positivity, and good vibes. When I stretch myself dangerously thin, they remind me to take a step back and slow down. Thanks also to my wonderfully supportive mother and sister, who listen to me drone on incessantly about my crafty endeavors without so much as one complaint.

I must also include acknowledgement to the crafters who follow and create along with me. To everyone who makes and shares my designs, I am truly indebted to you, and would not be here if it weren't for you. So from the bottom of my heart, I say thank you – I couldn't do it without such a loving community of spirited people who encourage me to create every day.

INDEX

A DAVID AND CHARLES BOOK

David and Charles is an imprint of David and Charles, Ltd
Suite A, Tourism House, Pynes Hill, Exeter, EX2 5WS

First published in the UK and USA in 2025

A catalogue record for this book is available from the British Library.

ISBN-13: 9781446315569 paperback
ISBN-13: 9781446315576 EPUB

This book has been printed on paper from approved suppliers and made from pulp from sustainable sources.

Printed in China through Asia Pacific Offset for:
David and Charles, Ltd
Suite A, Tourism House, Pynes Hill, Exeter, EX2 5WS

10 9 8 7 6 5 4 3 2 1

Publishing Director: Ame Verso
Senior Commissioning Editor: Sarah Callard
Managing Editor: Jeni Chown
Editor: Victoria Allen
Project Editors: Rachael Prest and Marie Clayton
Lead Designer: Sam Staddon
Designers: Jess Pearson and Nikki Ellis
Pre-press Designer: Susan Reansbury
Illustrations: Nikki Ellis
Technique Illustrations: Kuo Kang Chen
Art Direction: Sarah Rowntree
Photography: Jason Jenkins
Production Manager: Beverley Richardson